## *A Few Words to the Reader.*

THERE is no need for me to dilate on the qualities and work of my late revered friend, Rev. Thomas Lewis. Some who knew him well have put on record in this little volume what they thought of him. My task is a light and pleasant one—viz., that of assisting his daughter, Miss Lewis, to bring through the press the simple but interesting story of her father's life. Also his son, Mr. T. H. Lewis, has rendered valuable assistance. The man is clearly seen in this Autobiography—his simplicity, vivacity, diligence, straightforwardness, conscientiousness, and deep piety. God blessed him with a long life, good health, an excellent help-meet, dutiful children, and a host of friends, who could penetrate through his apparent brusqueness, and found within the genuine Christian and the true man. There is no need to recount his early struggles and difficulties, or to refer to his unquenchable thirst for knowledge, his praiseworthy diligence and unyielding perseverance in the pursuit of it; his high attainments in the original languages of Scripture, in theology, and other branches, especially when we consider his lack of advantages and the time he lived.

He possessed a memory that seemed capable of retaining anything—from Hebrew roots to innumerable dates and old-world incidents. He possessed the "historical imagination" that made him "live and move and have his being" among the heroes and saints of past centuries. He spoke of them as if he had conversed with them face to face. In every way his was a full, busy, pure, noble life. Having in his youth consecrated himself to the Lord's work, he kept right on, on the straight and ever upward road of service to the end. He possessed some of the noblest traits that could be discerned in any man, and there was a rare combination of excellences, which produced an *all-roundness*, and, so far as is possible on earth, a perfectness of character. His was a well-spent life, rich in labour, service, and abiding fruit. His course had not merely come to an end, but it "was finished." How much he did during a ministry which extended to more than fifty years! His industry was marvellous. Blessed with a good constitution, careful and temperate in his habits, he enjoyed good health, which enabled him to prosecute his work with vigour and freshness. He husbanded his time, and no precious portion was lost.

Being a man of great mental power, and possessing a most tenacious memory, coupled with unwearied diligence, it is no wonder that his acquirements were considerable. He was an excellent Hebrew scholar. He could read his Hebrew Bible with ease, and also his Greek Testament. He was also fairly proficient in Syriac, and very frequently he rendered great

# "MY LIFE'S HISTORY."

———

# THE AUTOBIOGRAPHY OF
# REV. THOMAS LEWIS.

THOMAS LEWIS.

# 'My Life's History.'

---

## THE AUTOBIOGRAPHY

OF

## REV. THOMAS LEWIS,

Baptist Minister, Newport (Mon.).

*(Together with short Notices from a few friends.)*

EDITED BY

## PRINCIPAL W. EDWARDS, D.D.,

SOUTH WALES BAPTIST COLLEGE, CARDIFF.

" Surely goodness and mercy have followed me all the days of my life."

---

## PRICE: TWO SHILLINGS NETT.

---

Newport (Mon.):
Published by (Miss) C. E. Lewis, 220, Chepstow Road.
Bristol:
W. Crofton Hemmons, St. Stephen Street.
1902.

service as an examiner in the various colleges. But as the historian of the denomination he was most noted. His mind was a store-house of facts. He was conversant with the history of the Baptists, especially in Wales, along the centuries; and the ease with which he remembered countless dates and events was astonishing. His translation of some of Spurgeon's sermons had a wide circulation. His brain and pen were ever busy, and the result of his labour will be an abiding boon to the churches. As a preacher, he was expository, intensely evangelical, practical, and earnest. As a pastor, he was faithful and impartial. He was a life-long, consistent advocate of Temperance, and set a noble example to all. As a citizen, he advocated strenuously equal rights for all in the State and in religion. He rendered great service as an enlightened educationalist. He was for years one of the secretaries of Pontypool College, and his counsel was ever highly valued.

His qualities of mind and heart endeared him to thousands. He possessed a frank, open nature, the main-spring of his life being in full view. His straightforwardness was ever to be admired. He spoke his mind, whether men would hear or whether they would forbear. It amounted at times to apparent bluntness; but there was no sting in any of his utterances, as there was no venom in his nature. Those who fully understood him were very much attached to him. His geniality was like the light, and his society like the refreshing breeze. He was a delightful companion. His homely wit, his apt

sayings, his fund of anecdote, his varied reminiscences, caused the hour to pass by as on the wing
of unmixed delight. And all was highly elevating.
His was a truly sanctified manhood: strength and
firmness were combined with a sweetness and lovable-
ness which were the fruit of the Spirit that dwelt in
him. He was a humble, devout Christian. The
Gospel of Christ was his all in all. His love to his
Saviour swayed his mind, and he lived to Him, served
Him with fidelity and success; and at the end of a
splendid life the Master said to him, " Come up
higher," and sweetly he suddenly fell asleep in His
strong and loving arms.

We send forth this little volume of record and
reminiscences, believing that it will be gladly received by the many friends that knew and respected
him, and that it will be read by many who did not
know him in the flesh as a memorial of a good, able,
and useful minister of the Gospel, and a loyal and a
most exemplary servant of the Lord Jesus Christ.

WM. EDWARDS.

SOUTH WALES BAPTIST COLLEGE,
    CARDIFF, *Dec.* 16*th*, 1901.

---

N.B.—The Autobiography is not divided into
chapters, but the *years* embraced in the record form
the "landmarks."

## *Brief Notices.*

### By Mr. David Williams, J.P., Carmarthen.

*A Few Facts relating to Rev. Thomas Lewis during his Ministry at Penuel, Carmarthen, from 1863 to 1874.*

HE was a strenuous and zealous advocate of unsectarian education. He laboured in season and out of season on behalf of the Lancastrian School, by serving on its board as one of its managers. He and the late Mr. Mortimer went around to collect the annual subscriptions towards the same. After the passing of the Act of 1870, the ecclesiastical Tories of Carmarthen exerted their utmost to prevent the establishing of a School Board in the town. The Vicar of St. Peter's—the late Rev. Latimer Jones—was a man of great ability and much influence, and he was the leader of the opposition. His party held many meetings in order to prevent the formation of a School Board, which Mr. Lewis almost invariably attended, as he with true courage accepted the challenge of the Vicar and his friends, and would ascend the platform, requesting the chairman to allow him to reply to the Vicar's statements, which reasonable request was not granted. But in spite of the bitter opposition, the friends of the people's schools succeeded in getting a School Board formed; and in securing this victory Mr. Lewis took a prominent part.

He was very successful in starting an English Baptist cause in the town, although it would deprive his church at Penuel of many of the richest families belonging to it. It is to be wondered at that the Rev. H. W. Jones was utterly indifferent or opposed to the formation of an English Baptist Church.

During his stay at Carmarthen Mr. Lewis showed considerable power as an *author*. While here his great work, "Esboniad y Teulu" ("The Family Commentary"), was published as far as the end of the Old Testament. He also edited a volume of the sermons of the Rev. James Richards, Pontypridd; he translated and published a volume of sermons by the Rev. C. H. Spurgeon; he published the Rev. Titus Lewis' Catechism; and he wrote a large number of articles to *Seren Gomer* and other Welsh periodicals.

His search for rare old books was unwearied. Whilst in North Wales, on one occasion, he came across a rare Hebrew Grammar written by Mr. Barker, who was tutor at the Carmarthen Grammar School towards the end of the eighteenth century. Some of that good man's descendants are still living in this town. When some of them came to know of the book, they were prepared to give any sum of money for it, but Mr. Lewis would on no consideration part with it; but he lent it to them for some time. When in the North, he would often be invited by Rev. T. Briscoe—a clergyman in Anglesea, I believe. He was afterwards appointed a Professor of Hebrew in Oxford University. When he was in Wales he published a new translation of the Prophecies of Isaiah into Welsh, with critical notes. It is no wonder that two Hebrew scholars enjoyed to the full each other's society.

When Mr. Lewis left for Monmouthshire, he was presented by the church and congregation with a gold watch and a purse of twenty sovereigns, as a slight token of sincere regard.

One of the impressions left on my mind is this: I never saw anyone so methodical and businesslike in whatever he undertook to do. His books and papers were so arranged as to be easily found. If one sat with him in his study and conversed with him about books, articles in magazines, etc., he could readily put his hand on whatever he wanted. His memory was most tenacious, and almost boundless. He was a "walking encyclopædia."

As a *Preacher*, he was simple and unassuming. He eschewed empty rhetoric and "swollen words." He clothed his strong, evangelical thought in simple, clear Welsh, and his delivery would often be full of fire, that would produce a deep impression.

As a *Pastor*, he was wonderfully straightforward, being no respecter of persons. When exercising church discipline, he would deal with the rich just as with the poorest member.

As a *Friend*, it would be impossible to find one more faithful and trustworthy. He was as attached to his old friends here after twenty years of separation as when he lived amongst them. I wrote many letters to him when he was at Newport, and I never found one more constant and true.

As a *Temperance Advocate*, he was earnest, consistent, and enthusiastic. He promoted, by all means in his power, total abstinence when it was unpopular to do so. He never sought to catch the popular breeze. He clung to the truth, for he loved it for its own sake. His piety was deep, his energy was unfailing, his diligence was marvellous, his conscientiousness was the main-spring of his conduct, and his service to his denomination and to the Church of Christ at large was inestimable.

## By Rev. W. Jones, Newport, Mon.

I am much pleased to understand that the Autobiography of the Rev. T. Lewis, late of Newport, is about to be published, not only because it contains the facts of his long, laborious, and very useful life, as Minister of the Gospel, Commentator, Historian, etc., but also facts relative to other public men, and the denomination in the Principality. A life nearly eighty years in length, of such a careful observer, such an incessant student, such an interesting talker and companion, such a diligent worker, such an excellent preacher and pastor, and such a bright character, must necessarily be of interest and value for ages, to those who can appreciate the good, the noble, and the beautiful.

It was at Pontypool on Wednesday, Oct. 12th, 1864, I first saw, and heard Mr. Lewis preach. And Mr. Parry, then of Cefnmawr, now Dr. Parry of Rhyl, happened to be in town the same day. Mr. Lewis had arranged to preach at the Tabernacle that evening; and as Mr. Parry came to the service, he also was requested to preach; and he consented. And as Mr. Parry was the younger man, he preached first. And it was a sermon on that familiar text, 1 *Tim.* i. 15, and characterized by much freshness and elaboration, and delivered in Mr Parry's happy and energetic style. Mr. Lewis followed him, taking for his text, *Eph.* iii. 8; and by the critical and interesting remarks which he made at the start on the peculiar expression in his text, "less than the least of all saints," he arrested the attentive hearing of the audience at once, and preached well, and with much effect. As he was a fairly good Hebrew and Greek scholar, he would often open up his text with some critical remarks, which would render his sermon throughout somewhat out of the common, yet very clear, and practical. Though perhaps he would not be generally regarded as belonging to the first rank of the preachers of his age in the Principality, yet, taking his life as a whole, in its manifold aspects, with all his varied and onerous labours, he must be regarded as one of the leading men in our denomination in Wales.

1. He was a man of very fine physique, healthy, strong, and vigorous in appearance. Though under

the average in height, he was unusually broad, his head unusually large, and his countenance indicating self-possession, firmness, and determination. And considering he was bulky and heavy, he used to walk very nimbly and lightly until a short time before his death.

2. His memory was wonderfully strong and retentive. He was naturally qualified to become a historian, antiquarian, and philologist, in which branches he also excelled. Though he was much devoted to study, and capable of wonderful application, it appears that he somewhat lacked in mental grasp, and spiritual insight, to become eminent as an expositor.

3. He was a hard, diligent, and persevering student. Were it not so he could never have succeeded in writing his Commentary on the whole Bible, with the exception of the four Gospels, and the Book of Revelation. And he wrote much besides, which required hard and diligent study, such as his pamphlets on baptism, biographical articles to the *Gwyddoniadur, Seren Gomer, Greal, etc.,* History of the Monmouthshire Baptist Churches, and many theological, expository, historical, and controversial articles, from time to time to the different Welsh Magazines, and Welsh and English Newspapers.

4. He excelled as an interesting talker and companion. Few ministers even can make themselves at home when from home, and among strangers, and interest a whole family for hours by what they say. Mr. Lewis used to do this in a very easy and natural way. He had such a store of facts treasured up in his

mind, and he was naturally and richly endowed with that unique power to relate facts, incidents, and circumstances in a very vivid and dramatic manner, so as to interest all listeners, children as well as adults. And he would never condescend to low talk, which has a tendency to demoralize the talker and the listeners ; but as a rule he would relate facts, incidents, and circumstances, which he had witnessed within the sphere of the religious life, either connected with church work, old ministers, preaching services, or associations. Many a time I spent two or three hours with him in his study, and always felt sorry, on my way home, I could not write the interesting facts, with the dates and circumstances, as he had just related them to me.

5. Moreover, he was very generous and kind. I found him a friend in need when in troubles and difficulties. And he was a very ready contributor to any good cause. He would speak with honesty, straightforwardness, and severity in condemnation of any wrong, yet he was as ready as any one to be kind to the wrong-doer.

6. To crown all he was a man of very bright character. He was a total abstainer for about sixty years, and did a great deal privately, and publicly, to advocate the Temperance Movement. And hence he would never be found among the low and suspected class. I hope his autobiography will be widely circulated and read, and his life as represented therein, will lead and stimulate many to labour diligently and earnestly for Christ, always abounding in the work of

the Lord, knowing their labour shall not be in vain in the Lord.

### By Rev. T. G. James, Tydu, Mon.

In our appreciation of the Rev. Thomas Lewis, the public must not expect a character sketch, nor our impressions in outline form of him as a writer, preacher, historian, and scholar. Sufficient will it be for me to say that he honoured and adorned all these important branches. Thomas Lewis (for by that name he was known, and so will he be remembered) was one of the most interesting characters of his day. In his company time flew. Well do we remember the very first time we saw him in the flesh (by name he was familiar before, especially to my parents, as the author of "Esboniad y Teulu") : it was during the week of my entrance examination, on the lawn before Pontypool College, talking to the Revs. Evan Thomas (Newport) and S. R. Young (Abergavenny). Fourteen years have passed since then. My first impression was, his spotless cleanliness—he was always well groomed.

After my settlement at Bethesda, Tydu, we obtained facilities to come into very close contact one with another, for he was a member here ever since he resigned the pastorate of Moriah, Risca. Besides, he had other duties which demanded frequent visits to the district, and seldom would he come out without calling on the writer. Unless fulfilling preaching engagements or unwell, he would invariably be present at our monthly Communion. Thomas Lewis shone in many directions, but I believe that he was never better than when speaking of the "infinite love of Jesus" at the Communion table. Thomas Lewis made this portion of our services memorable, inspiring, and soul-elevating. He knew Jesus well. His homely addresses often reminded me of that beautiful little story, "Vida Amy Dunsmuir." There is a little talk between Vida and her playfellow. "There is a God." "How do you know that?" "Because," said Vida, "I know someone who knows Him: Mr. Jeffrey does. One Sunday last summer Mr. Jeffrey preached for papa. It was then that he told us about God. It was not the least like *preaching;* it was telling us things that he really knew, you know." "And you think Mr. Jeffrey believes in God, Vida?" "It isn't that he *believes in Him,* Arthur; he knows Him as you know me. I think he knows Him better than anyone else, for he is very shy with other people. If Mr. Jeffrey went to London and preached to those people you speak about, they would see that there must be a God."

Thomas Lewis knew his Father and his Saviour well. There was a ring of certainty in his voice which helped you to feel the Rock under your feet. His friendship will ever remain fragrant; from him we learnt many a lesson. He was of the Puritan type. I remember him coming into my study once flaming in righteous wrath. It was election time, and he had written a letter to the local press on "Protestantism," and the editor remarked that it would alienate the Catholic vote. The policy of putting policy before principle riled him immensely. "Such actions," he remarked, "I simply detest!" So the letter never appeared.

During the last five years of his life he lived a great deal in the past. In his honest opinion there were no days like the good old days of long ago. Perhaps he was, after all, correct.

The closing months of his life revealed to those who frequently met him, and spent some time in his company, a richness, freshness, and mellowness of character of a rare and exquisite type—waiting for the Master's call without the least tremor. Even death had no terror.

I believe it was a month before he died when he casually remarked and carried on the following conversation: "Look here, Brother James. I think that I have been of some little service in the Master's vineyard during my lifetime, but I cannot establish a claim for Heaven on that. I have tried, but it gives way—it's shaky—there is no firmness in it, no pleading power. I know my Bible fairly well," he further remarked, "but there is only one verse upon which I love to lean, and with which I love to dwell: 'He that believeth on the Son hath everlasting life.' I have no other hope; if that fails, I am lost. But *I do believe*, and I know that I am safe."

Sleep, brother, sleep. Rest, brother, rest. A life well spent. A race nobly run. Thou art in good company: Dudley Evans is close by, Evan Thomas is also near—two of Gwalia's brightest pulpit stars. The trumpet shall sound, and you pulpit heroes shall arise.

BY REV. SIDNEY R. YOUNG, ABERGAVENNY.

At the time of my ministerial settlement in this town in 1856, Rev. Thomas Lewis was the pastor of the neighbouring church of Llanthewy Rhytherch, where he had been doing good and steady work for some time. From my personal acquaintance with many of the members of the church, I am able to say that he was held in high respect, and his ministry was conscientiously discharged and fully appreciated. In the country, and before the rush and hurry of life within and outside the church had set in, and many questionable methods of carrying on the cause of Christ had been discovered and adopted, consuming time and not increasing spirituality, Mr. Lewis was able to devote a large share of his time to the prosecution of Classical and Biblical studies. He used to set apart one day a week to keeping up his acquaintance with classical authors, and the Greek Testament and Hebrew Bible were not long out of his hands. His attainments in this direction were considerable, and put many of us into the shade. His preaching was deeply evangelical, his discourses simple in arrangement, and delivered oftentimes with energy and effect. He rendered excellent service to the denomination by his writings in our Welsh periodicals, as well as by Biblical works of a highly useful character. He also served the interests of our college, now located in Cardiff—though he was one of those who regretfully saw its removal from Pontypool—as one of the secretaries, and on several occasions as an examiner. The proceedings at the college annual meetings and at committee meetings were greatly assisted by the wide and accurate knowledge which he exhibited of the churches of Wales, his fair-mindedness and sound judgment, and were often enlivened by his quaint remarks and "dry" humour. Mr. Lewis' character, all through his life, was above reproach, and his usefulness continued to the last, his relinquishment of the pastorate leaving him free to serve various churches seeking his ministrations, while his pen was busy as formerly. The memory of Thomas Lewis will be kindly cherished by his ministerial and other brethren; and of him it may truly be said, that "he was a good man, and feared God above many."

## My Ancestors.

MY grandfather, Thomas Lewis, lived at a farm called Cwmyronen (of which he was the owner), in the parish of Llanfair-ar-y-bryn in the County of Carmarthen. His will, which I have in my possession, was proved February 28th, 1818, on the oath of his widow, Anne Lewis.

My grandmother was an Independent, and a member at Cefnarthen; but in her last years she was a Baptist. The old people were buried at their Parish Church, Llanfair-ar-y-bryn; but I was never able to find their grave.

Thomas and Anne Lewis had two sons and one daughter—Daniel Lewis, my father, was the eldest. Joseph Lewis, my uncle, married and lived at Cwmyronen after his mother; Ruth, the only daughter, was married to one William Davies. They were members at Cefnarthen to the end of their life: they have a large number of their descendants in that neighbourhood.

My father, his brother Joseph, and their mother were among the first members at Horeb, Cwmdwr. Joseph was a very godly man, and died in the prime of life, on May 16th, 1828, aged 36 years: he was buried at Horeb. He left a widow and children. From his elegy, written by Thomas Thomas, Cwmdwr, it appears that he was baptized at Horeb in 1820. This Thomas Thomas became a minister, and died when pastor of the Tabernacle Baptist Church, Merthyr Tydfil.

My father also was a member at Horeb from 1820 till his sudden death, December 22nd, 1852, aged 65 years. He had a good share of the troubles of this world, but I have reason for believing that he now rests with Christ.

My mother, whose maiden name was Margaret Evans, was from the Parish of Llywel, Breconshire. I knew nothing of her parents, save this—that they were buried at Llywel with this short record on their grave :—" Thomas Evans of this parish, Joan his wife : She died May 26th, 1820, ae. 70. He died Jan. 17th, 1821, ae. 81."

My mother spent the first part of her life with her uncle, William Jones, a small farmer at Waunlwyd, in the parish of Llandilo'r fan. There my father and mother first lived after their marriage (March 5th, 1822), and then I was born on August 3rd, 1823. From there they removed to a larger adjoining farm named Trelâth. In a very few years my parents gave up farming and removed to Cwmdwr, where, after many years, they finished their earthly sojourn.

My father had learnt saddlery, which he followed after giving up the farm. My mother was a very industrious woman, and laboured hard to bring up a family of five children—three of whom have long passed away. She was also a member at Horeb, and very consistent : remarkable for her faithfulness, meekness, and prayerfulness. After much weakness and suffering, she died December 17th, 1853, aged 73 years.

My dear parents, two sisters and a brother rest together at Horeb : the spot is marked by a head-stone which I had placed there when I was a minister at Carmarthen.

Although I was only 5 or 6 years old when my parents removed from Trelath to Cwmdwr, yet I remember some things that occurred there—*e.g.* cutting turf for fuel—a cottage being burned down—the discovery of sulphur water.

But what impressed me most was, the first religious meeting I ever attended : it was held at the next farm, called Pantybrynshwn. (That old house disappeared long ago—the last time I passed that way I could scarcely discover the site of it.)

The house was full of people; there was much praising (*molianu*), lifting of hands, and some "jumping." That meeting impressed me very much : even now I remember the hymn they were singing :—

> " Gwell yw myn'd trwy orthrymderau
>     Mewn i dir y bywyd draw," etc.
> (" Better pass through tribulations
>     To the land of yonder life," etc.)

There was a general revival in Wales from 1827 to 1829 (see a long letter on this from Rev. D. Peter, of Carmarthen, to Rev. Caleb Morris, London, in the "Bap. Miscellany," 1829, p. 205). The eminent W. Williams, of Pantycelyn, the great hymnist of Wales, defended "jumping" in the time of revivals. To a man who objected to it, he said: There lived on the same side of a hill two men and one woman who had commenced life about the same time: their names were Evan, Thomas, and Betty. Each had borrowed £100 to begin business, and had hoped ere long to be able to repay their loans: in that they failed, and a law suit was threatened. Eventually the bailiffs came, and Evan was taken to prison. As he was passing with his captors by the house of Sir John Goodman on the other side of the hill, Sir John met them, and said, "Evan, where art thou going?" "Well, sir," said Evan, "I am going to prison for debt; I owe the money, but cannot pay, and I have no hope of ever getting out of prison." "I am indeed sorry to hear," said Sir John. "How much is the debt?" "It is £100 besides costs." "Well, Evan," said Sir John, "I will pay that debt"; and he said to the bailiffs, "I bind myself to pay the debt—let him go free." It is not easy to conceive the joy and gratitude of Evan for this. As he was returning home, and had come to the brow of the hill above his house, he shouted with all his might, "Thanks, thanks to Sir John Goodman." Betty heard and saw him, greatly wondered and thought he was mad. She went up to him to know the cause, and when he had told her, she joined him and shouted, "Thanks, thanks to Sir John Goodman. Afterwards, Thomas saw and heard them: he went up to know the reason of all the noise: when he was told, he also shouted, "Thanks, thanks, thanks to Sir John Goodman." The point of the parable was—to show

how great a cause had those, whose sins were pardoned, to leap for joy. (Life of Rowlands, of Llangeitho," by Rev. Jas. Owen, p. 98.)

As there was no chapel at Trelâth, the only chance I had of a meeting was one now and again in some house. The few people around were Independents and Calvinistic Methodists; my parents were the only Baptists. I well remember them going to Cwmdwr on Sundays: father used to walk, and mother rode; they had about four miles to go.

*At Cwmdwr.*—Here I remember going to Horeb for the first time in my life. I was much interested both in the crowd of people and the preaching. The minister at the time, and for many years, was the good Thomas Williams, formerly of Cwmdu, county of Carmarthen. He died in 1861, age 76; was buried at Zoar. Though I had not had any schooling before this time, yet I had learned to read Welsh in the old "Welshman's Candle." At this time a day school was opened at Horeb Chapel by Mr. Thos. Jones, of Crugybwbach. (He subsequently became a clergyman, and died at a good age.) That was the first school I ever attended. After Mr. Jones, the school was carried on by Mr. Henry Phillips, a Baptist preacher. I was in his school a good while. I have now an English Bible which I used at that time, and Mr. Phillips has written in it, in a good hand: "Thos. Lewis's book; March 12th, 1834. Henry Phillips, teacher, Horeb." Mr. Phillips died in old age at Nantyglo; he was a member at Hermon. During the years I was at Cwmdwr I worked now and again at the wool factory which was kept by Mr. Griffith Wilson, and after him by Mr. Edward Evans. Both were Independents. I also worked a few months at Pont-ar-ydfer factory, near Cwmwysg. That was kept by Mr. Joshua Davies, a Calvinistic Methodist. He was a member at Trecastle, and precentor; was a very good singer, and often kept evening schools for teaching music.

Two boys like myself worked at the factory. One was Edward Thomas, now a clergyman at Skewen, near Neath. The other was the well-known John Davies, who became a prominent man among the Independents. He ministered at Llanelly, Brecon, Aberaman, and at Cardiff, where he died. Though small and weak in body, yet he had a most active soul, and he attained to great eminence.

After the departure of Mr. Henry Phillips from Cwmdwr, the school was conducted by Mr. William Jenkins (son of Rev. Peter Jenkins, once minister at Brychgoed), in whose school I was both at Horeb and Pentretygwyn. To and from the latter place I had to walk six miles, morning and evening. Mr. W. Jenkins has written on the last page of my Bible that I was at his school in 1835.

I was baptized at Cwmdwr by Rev. Thomas Williams on June 4th, 1837, being then fourteen years of age.

From Cwmdwr I went to Llanwrtyd Wells, where I worked in Mr. Winston's wool factory for six months. I then returned to my parents, who sent me to Madam Bevan's school, kept by the well-known Mr. David Owen (*Brutus*). That school was kept at an old toll-gate called Gatfach, near Pentrebach. I was there about eighteen months, and then returned to Mr. Winston's, where I worked till the end of 1842. While there I became a member at Pantycelyn, under the ministry of Rev. Richard Hughes.

During the time I was at Llanwrtyd I witnessed two great Revivals: many jumping, singing, and praying from the chapel to their homes, till their voices had entirely failed. I myself sang so much once that I lost my speech for two days. There was no "jumping" among the Baptists, but great earnestness and life. Rev. D. Williams, of Gelynos, was very powerful at that time. While he was preaching I saw men jump so much that the preacher had to sit down and let the people have their way. There was much power attending the meetings, and very many were saved. I saw young men and women coming to meetings for fun, but going away singing and praying. But there was *some* chaff. There was intense earnestness in those days. I remember that, following the Sunday I was baptized, the Baptist Association was held at Watergate, Brecon, on the Tuesday and Wednesday. Full of youthful zeal, I attended it, walking fifteen miles there and back the second evening, I being then under fourteen years old. That was my first Association, with the exception of the Calvinistic Methodist Association at Trecastle.

*Temperance.*—When I went to Llanwrtyd I found that Temperance was shaking the whole place. There was *dirwest* in every meeting and in every sermon, and no account was taken of any Christian unless he was a Temperance man. There were also processions with music and banners. Robin Ddu was a prominent man, although after that he greatly disappointed his friends.

At that time I joined the teetotalers, and I hold on to the present time—now more than fifty years. It is safe ground, and I rejoice in it. Had I not been a total abstainer, I have reason to believe I would have been intemperate, if not worse.

Mr. Winston and his family were very religious. Family worship, both morning and evening, would never be thrust aside. It mattered not how busy we were, or what time of the year it might be. Mr. Winston, his son, myself, "Shemi," John Price, Jack, and Nathaniel had to engage in our turn. The two old farm labourers could not read, so someone else read, and they had to pray, which they did very well. The whole family were about thirty in number. Mr. Winston had about fourteen children. He kept a factory, a fulling-mill, and a large farm; but religion was never set aside. All attended meetings and Sunday schools regularly; no one was allowed to keep away.

I had commenced preaching before I left Llanwrtyd. I went to Cwmdwr to begin; but it was at Pantycelyn that I spoke first in public, at a farm-house called Bryn-arth-goch. My first text was from *Deut.* xxxii. 31, and my second *Eph.* v. 2. I began to preach about the latter part of 1840.

From my childhood I was much exercised about preaching. I preached many times before I was fourteen. I used to preach in the wood and quarries at Cwmdwr. I preached often in the pulpit at Horeb when I could get the chapel to myself. I also preached in the loft of the factory on Sunday afternoons while at Mr. Winston's. "Shemi" (or Jas. Williams), Mr. Winston's farm servant, was with me, and tried his hand at preaching, but could make no headway. He was a good man, and a Methodist, but had to give up all thoughts of *cynghori* (exhorting).

The ministers whom I heard in the early part of my life were the following :—

## BAPTIST MINISTERS.

1. Morgan Lewis of Chapelyffin, or Morgan Lewis of Brynmelyn, as he was called. I thought that he was an excellent preacher; and I am under the impression that it was him I heard first, and that was at Horeb on a warm Sunday morning. He was at Abergavenny Academy, and was ordained in 1825. He died April 2nd, 1887, aged 90.

2. David Jones, Cwmsarnddu. He was a farmer— a strong man with a powerful voice. The people were glad to hear him. When he had warmed up he would say to the people: "Shall I shout? Let the Crown be on His head!" Putting the hand to the ear, you could hear him far away.

3. John Morgan, of Talyryn, near Llandovery. He was brought up as a gentleman; was a scholar, having studied under Dr. Ryland at Bristol. He was an esquire and a magistrate, and all looked up to him.

He was a very able preacher. His last pastorate was at the Baptist Church, Llandovery.

4. John Williams, Llandovery, was the reverse of Mr. Morgan. He was a shoemaker, rather poor; yet he was a thoughtful preacher, though not popular. He was an amiable brother, and godly beyond a doubt. I called to see him several times when he was ailing, and near his end.

5. James Davies. He had been minister at Pantycelyn, was a very effective preacher, and to the last popular in the Churches. He went to America from Tabor, Brynmawr, in his old age, and there he died.

6. R. Hughes, Pantycelyn. He was not popular, although full of matter. He died at Verwig, near Cardigan. He was a good man. I heard him several times.

7. Rowland Peter, from Carnarvonshire. He supplied at Pantycelyn after the departure of R. Hughes. Old Rowland was eccentric and original; his knowledge of the Bible and of Wales was extensive. He was at Pantycelyn about six months.

8. J. P. Williams. He was ordained at Pantycelyn, became very popular, and died young at St. Dogmell's.

9. John Jones, of Sardis, was from Pembrokeshire. He was a farmer. He was fluent in speech, although not an able man.

10. David Arthur, of Erwood. A good old man, who began to preach in middle age. He was unrivalled in prayer. I heard him pray on a Sunday evening at Llangorse, in the year 1843, till the whole congregation was overcome; even the ungodly wept beyond any-

thing I had ever witnessed. His preaching and mine, after that prayer, were as nothing.

11. Benjamin Williams, of Maesyberllan. Quite a gentleman, and the most popular minister in the county.

12. John Evans, of Brecon. He spent his long life in the one church. An able man, but not sympathetic. He went very little from home. He refused to sign my application to college, although requested by his dear friend, T. Williams, Cwmdwr; his reason being that he had never heard me preach.

13. Thomas Roberts, Pontestyll, near Brecon. A very good man, and a scholar. He kept school at times, and was a refined preacher, but far ahead of his hearers.

During the years I was at Winston's I used to go often to Pantycelyn, four or five miles away. Many a Sunday I had walked 20 miles by the time I reached home, as the services were held in different places—at Chapel in the morning and at farm-houses at two and six. Sometimes I would go on Sundays to the distant Churches of Sardis and Zoar Llanfihangel, returning home to rest, as I had to be at work at six on Monday morning. The longest journey was to Bwlchyrhiw and Rhandirmwyn in 1842. I started on Sunday morning at four o'clock by Llanwrtyd Church: thence to Cwmhenog, where I had a guide over the mountain. I preached twice that day, and returned by 10 or 11 at night.

I happened, for the first time, to meet Rees Price at Bwlchyrhiw, and preached with him there on Sunday morning. He spent his ministerial life at Cilfowyr, where he died, July 12th, 1896, aged 75. (See Cardiff College Register, p. 215.)

## INDEPENDENT MINISTERS.

1. Jenkin Morgan, Pentretygwyn, was an old man when I was very young : he died in 1833, aged 72 years. He was very plain, yet very earnest ; sometimes he could be heard half-a-mile away. I remember being at Cwmllwyfog on a Sunday afternoon, and could hear him preaching at John the Tailor's house at Doldowns —fully half-a-mile distant !

2. Edward Jones—he succeeded J. Morgan in the pastorate at Pentre and Cefnarthen : he was a very humble man and a prosperous minister. He died early of consumption : I called to see him on his death-bed, in 1841.

3. David Evans, Cwmwysg. He was a plain farmer, and a preacher of the warm old style. Mr. T. Williams, Cwmdwr, and he used to exchange pulpits ; he died in 1863, aged 76.

4. David Williams, Llanwrtyd. He was wonderfully popular—and deservedly so. Insignificant in person, but a giant in the pulpit ; he often carried everything like a flood before him. He died at the great age of 97 : I heard him at the age of 91 at Carmarthen.

5. D. Davis, of Sardis, was a very sweet preacher : he died when I was young, still I remember him well.

## CALVINISTIC METHODISTS.

I heard many of them during my term of service with Mr. Winston.

1. Thomas Elias—very sensible and solid; he was much respected by all, and he deserved it. He had a brother, named Elias Elias, who was a deacon at the " Bont "; he was always very friendly with me, and more liberal than any I found in those days. Though I was a Baptist, Elias loved me, and was ready to help me. Through his introduction I preached more than once in the Methodist Chapel at the " Bont."

2. Ebenezer Williams. His father, "Daffy" Williams, was a good old man, full of the spirit of Llangeitho. He used to carry drapery about the country, especially women's apparel.

At the time of the Great Revival a young woman, handsome and proud, named Nannie, came before the Church. "Daffy" spoke to her, and among other things said, " Nannie, you must now be different from what you were before; you must not be proud and dressy, and wear all these ribbons in bunches about your head." She replied, " Well, what am I to do? I bought them of you, and if I shan't wear them, why do you sell them, and even force them upon me? " Of course, poor " Daffy " was dumb, and sat down.

Ebenezer Williams was a fair preacher: at one time he became insane, and at mid-day in summer ran naked through the village, being caught with difficulty. However, he was restored, and ministered to the end of his life at Brecon.

3. William Havard. A great man in his day: popular, but very heavy, like his person; he was quite a load to a strong animal. His son, a minister at

C

Tredwstan, was very much like him, and weighed fully 21 stone.  I knew him very well.

4. William Morris, St. David's.  He was a melting preacher.  I cannot forget his sermon at Trecastle in 1844, on Paul's Voyage to Rome (*Acts* xxvii. 27): "The shipmen deemed that they drew nigh to some country."  O, the unction and feeling!  This I know, that I was full of joy, though shedding tears all the time.

5. Thomas Richards, Fishguard: him I heard many times.  Very majestic in his velvet cap, and very powerful at times.  I heard him at Llandovery Association, about 1840, and at his best.  The people sang for a long time after the sermon, the old preacher holding on with them for about half-an-hour in a most melodious voice.  Some of the people began to leap about me in the square, for there the Association was held.  The tune was "Delyn Aur" (*Golden Harp*), and the words that fired were these, "Mae dy gariad heb ddim dechreu" (Blessed Love, without beginning!) etc.  The line "Mae dy gariad uwch nas clywodd neb erioed" (Love eternal, nobler than the highest strain), was sung for a long time: it was good to be there.

6. John Evans, New Inn.  A fine, tall man, very absent in mind, and generally losing his way in travelling.  I remember him being stopped both at prayer and sermon on a Sunday afternoon at Gorwydd.  He would not end his prayer till stopped, nor the sermon till a sign was made: he would forget all about time in his theme.  He was a great preacher.  When at Mr. Winston's they failed to get him out of bed in

time for 10 o'clock service at "The Bont," and it was with some difficulty they got him off in time for Gorwydd in the afternoon. His text then was, "And Thou wilt cast all their sins into the depths of the sea." He had five "heads," and said "secondly" when it was four o'clock. Of course he was stopped: "Jack Bryrffo" went up to the pulpit, pulled the tail of his coat, and the great man was silenced at once. He had barely time to go to Llangammarch, where he was to preach at six o'clock.

7. Henry Rees. I heard him several times: first, at Trevecca, when the College was opened. Of him I need not write.

8. William Evans, of Tonyrefail, I heard more than 46 years ago. He was preaching until 91 years of age, and died in 1890.

I had no acquaintance with Wesleyans, nor with any of the clergy, except Rev. D. Parry, of Llywel: he was an excellent preacher, and was always kind to me; and I have several letters from him. Had the majority of the clergy been like him the Church of England would be crowded and Dissent at a discount.

Having saved a few pounds I went to a Grammar School at Tredwstan, near Trevecca, in January, 1843, my object being to prepare for some college. The master was Rev. David Williams, the minister of the chapel, a good and kind man. I was there (off and on) for about nine months. In the summer of that year I made a tour in North Wales, and preached in very many chapels. That journey did me good, as I became more free from timidity, which aforetime had nearly crushed me. I was from home several weeks. I walked from Breconshire to Anglesea and back, preaching every night and twice or thrice on Sundays. Great was the Lord's mercy towards me! Mr. Prichard, Llangollen, well-nigh sent me home (see his Memoir, p. 338, by O. Davies, Carnarvon).

When in Anglesea I preached at Amlwch, and slept at the house of the well-known Mr. Palmer. I preached at the chapel from *Ps.* cvii. 8, "Oh that men," &c. The sermon so pleased some of the family that they made me at once promise to copy it for the Cardiff *Bedyddiwr*, which I did next day before leaving the house. The editor acknowledged the manuscript on the cover of the next *Bedyddiwr*, and I never heard more about it. That sermon passed well several times on my journey, but I have no copy of it as far as I can find. The verse is marked in my Bible, but no further reference to the MS., which has, no doubt, perished with many others.

After my return I worked at Senny Bridge Factory for a few weeks with Mr. Joshua Davies. I had previously worked for him at the old factory at Pont-ar-ydfer. Mr. Davies was a Methodist, and a good singer. In that year (1844) I published a translation of Mr. Crapps' tract on Baptism; sold a few hundred copies of it, and thus had some help to go to college. But I found it difficult to get admitted, and was on the point of returning to my trade, and clinging to the factory for life. But it was otherwise ordained. I was admitted to Pontypool College, January 6th, 1845.

Here I may pause and wonder! No one could have begun lower. I was helpless among a people who had, at least, no money to help me, and I had to strive on and help myself as best I could. I had plenty of good wishes—but nothing more. Brought up, also, in the heart of the country, I had neither knowledge nor manners—save Bible knowledge and natural simplicity. Yet the Invisible Hand led me on step by step, till I found myself under the guidance of those good men, Revs. Thomas Thomas and George Thomas, whose memory to me is precious.

I spent three profitable years in college, and passed as well as I could through the course.

[When at College I sent an article on "Demons" to *Seren Gomer*; also a few pieces to *Tyst Apostolaidd* (1847): *vide* "Piety" (poetry), p. 52; "Melchisedek," p. 239; "A Reply," p. 196; "Poetry," p. 246. See a paper on "Doethineb Duw," in *Seren Gomer* (1846), p. 104. See also, "William Tell," pp. 172, 204, 372, part of which was translated by a fellow-student named T. Edred Jones, who died in America.]

During my college course I went, like other students, to collect throughout the churches. In 1845 I collected in the Old Association, Brecon, Radnor, and Montgomery shires. It was hard work, as I travelled all on foot and preached about eight times a week. Some of the journeys were long, lonely, and rough! In 1846 I had Carmarthen, Cardigan, and part of Pembroke shires, involving very laborious and hard walking. My partner soon broke down, and I had to do nearly all. I was out for ten weeks instead of two months—the usual time.

In 1847 the work was much lighter, as I had only parts of Monmouthshire. I learned at the outstart of my life what hardship meant, but the kind Lord helped as the heed arose—praise for ever to Him!

At the end of my term I was asked to supply the church at Amlwch, and also the Welsh Church in Manchester—with a view—but, receiving a call from Llanthewy, near Abergavenny, I accepted; and commenced my ministry there on January 9th, 1848. The salary paid me was £37 a year, and I do not think I was worth more! My predecessor, Rev. Daniel Jones, never had even that. I think his stipend was £24 a year.

The cause at the time was very low. There had been ill feelings, the fragments and embers of which still remained. My ordination took place on the 12th and 13th of April following. I was honoured with the presence of most worthy ministers:—Revs. Edward Evans, Penygarn; Thos. Thomas, the Tutor; D. D. Evans, Pontrhydyrun; and Francis Hiley, Llanwenarth. At the ordination I was asked to make some statements bearing upon myself and the ministry, and here follows what I had written for the occasion. [From this point in my history to the end I shall have the advantage of full records and diaries, which I have kept. Of course, I shall have to compress and omit, as I have volumes of notes, extending from 1848 down to the present year.]

Dr. Thomas propounded three questions: 1 (Q.) What proofs have you that you are a true Christian? (A.) Being a constant hearer of the Gospel, and a diligent reader of God's Word, before I was 10 years of age my attention was directed to these great truths: That it is appointed for all men once to die, and that all are unprepared to meet the Judge. I was terrified in view of eternity. I found that I was lost for anything I could do! In this state of mind I delighted to read of Christ, who came to seek and to save the lost. Soon I concluded that there was no salvation apart from Him. Once I never trusted in God's dear Son; but, thinking of His marvellous goodness, I was constrained to love Him and keep His commandments. I yielded obedience to Him in Baptism, and was received into His Church. While determined to hold out to the end, yet I was in great fear lest I should backslide. It was my daily prayer that I might be kept from the evils of this life, and from falling. I rejoiced greatly in the prosperity of the Gospel, and was grieved when any disgraced the religion of Christ. I loved the house of God more and more, and could say, "Lord, I love the habitation of Thy house, the place where Thine honour dwelleth."

2. (Q.) What proofs have you that you are called to the ministry? (A.) My mind was occupied with thoughts of preaching even before I was baptized—then not quite 13. I said nothing to any of the members about what was in my mind until 3 years after I was baptized. I was so troubled with preaching-thoughts, that I prayed daily for their removal if it

was not the will of God that I should be one of His messengers. I did my best to get rid of those thoughts, that I might have quiet to follow my trade, in which I had taken great delight. Instead of decreasing, however, they greatly increased in power and intensity. At last I had to decide for the ministry, come what would of it. I reasoned thus :—The Gospel must be preached, and that by men—old ministers are dying and new ones must take their place; and though feeble, yet through God they can do great things. I thought further, that if God intended me for the ministry, it would be wicked to disobey Him ; and if that obedience devolved on me, woe unto me if I preach not the Gospel. At length I yielded, believing that it was God's will that I should be placed in the ministry. I had no thought of worldly gain; my desire was that I might preach salvation to the lost, and win sinners to Christ. When I consider all things, and look around me, it is my belief that God has been pleased to call me into the service of His Kingdom.

3. (Q.) What are the doctrines you believe, and intend to preach and defend in your public ministry ? (A.) I believe that the Bible contains the whole of God's revelation to man : here we read of the Eternal God, the Maker and Sustainer of all things. He made man in His own image ; but man fell, and the race is lost. God, however, had foreseen all, and had provided a Saviour from Eternity. He sent His Son to die for us, that all believers in Christ may live for ever. Christ ascended into Heaven, where He has all authority above and below.

His Gospel must be preached to all men; and we must pray for the help of the Spirit that the Gospel may conquer those who hear it. Believers ought to be immersed in water in the name of the Father, Son and Holy Ghost. The other ordinance is the Lord's Supper: this, and all that Christ commands, must be observed by His followers. True Christians shall never perish, but shall have rest with Christ in glory. But unbelievers shall be condemned, and sent away from Christ and His Saints. Our churches are independent of each other, and all contributions must be voluntary.

This is a brief statement of my views: I pray that I may be enlightened more and more, and that I may delight in God's law at all times. (April 14th, 1848.)

During the year I sent a few papers to the *Tyst Apostolaidd; vide* " Heathen Mythology," pp. 238, 257, 279 and (1849) pp. 13, 35. In 1848, Questions, p. 207, and Poetry, p. 233.

Dec., 1848.—Here is one year more of my life gone, and the first for me as a Christian minister. I find that the work is great. In the first part of the year I felt happy, but after that I was much cast down for want of success; not one was baptized in the year! Everything, however, was calm and peaceable, the congregation has been good, and increases. This, with the kindness of the people, and an inward witness of sincerity, have held me up in many a dark hour. May the coming year be better! O Lord, revive Thy Church; may the people live more to Thee, and less to the world. This year has been remarkable for the deadness of all Christian work. It was also *Annus Mirabilis* as to the great political changes on the Continent.

During this year I sent a few papers to the *Tyst Apostolaidd :* Poetry, p. 233; Questions, p. 207; "Heathen Mythology," pp. 238, 257, 279.

1849.—This year has been remarkable for cholera epidemic in England and Wales. Thousands have died from the disease, which caused a panic among the people—the mere hearers of the Word. Many hundreds fled to the churches for membership, especially on the hills and in the ironworks. It is feared that terror only has driven many, and not the constraining love of Christ.

No great changes have occurred in this neighbourhood; the state of religion is much the same. Many come to chapel, but all continue just as before. I baptized one—an old man, who was my first candidate. Though he was stiff and heavy, all passed off decently, and the wicked had nothing to jeer at.

How is it that there is no prosperity in this little church? Many of the brethren appear to pray earnestly. Lord, Thou knowest what hinders. Remove it speedily, wherever it may be. Is it in me? Oh, teach me to pray; help me to preach with all earnestness. Pour upon us Thy good Spirit. Lord, remember me soon, for Thy name's sake. I bless Thee for helping me when about to despair, and when I feared my life would soon end.

I had melancholy thoughts for months, and my life had become a burden. Those miserable thoughts are now gone, and may they never return! I have determined to work more than ever. I will go and visit the people—members, hearers, and others who hear not; I will try what can be done in that way. I will talk the Gospel to the faces of the people at their homes. May God help me, and may I personally be more influenced by that Gospel which I preach to others!

Oct. 5.—I received a grant of books from the London Baptist Fund; among others, I have the works of President Edwards and Andrew Fuller. I have read their memoirs: they were the "excellent of the earth."

Oct. 14 (Sunday).—Had a good day, especially at six o'clock. The Lord smiled upon us. There is nothing so sweet as God's love to sinners. O Lord, bless Thy Word to those who heard it. Let me dwell at Thy feet, near the Cross; for that is the place that suits me and my sort.

Oct. 21 (Sunday).—I preached this morning on the work of grace in the soul. May I know more about it! In the evening I preached on David's love to God's house. May I experience greater delight in Thy service!

Oct. 27 (Saturday night).—Have returned from the preparatory meeting. My spirit is cast down. I am afraid I shall see no good in this place. How hard the people! Brotherly love is very scarce. One is offended—is so touchy—more like glass than gold. Another thinks he is not noticed enough—is not asked to read and pray more frequently. How can one deal with such people? It will not do to be harsh—though often tempted to dash the tables, as Moses did.

There were but few present at this meeting. The Sabbath meetings are fairly well attended, but few come to our prayer meetings. How careless many of the members are! What wonder that the hearers are indifferent, and that there is no prosperity! O my God! what ought I to do? Shall I resign?—must I leave the place and the people in their misery? Oh, have mercy on us all, and send prosperity! Save! save! save! and that quickly. Be with me on the morrow. Let the love of Christ possess my soul as I approach His table.

Oct. 28 (Sunday).—Good all day; great many present. When I am weak, I am strong. I never realised that more than to-day.

Nov. 4 (Sunday).—Had good meetings all day, but not up to the mark. I want to feel more of the importance of preaching. This week we purpose holding prayer meetings for a revival in the church. O Lord, be near us, and answer us in Thy great mercy.

Nov. 11 (Sunday).—A young man preached in the morning, and I in the evening. Very good service; never had more freedom. "The Coming of the Shiloh" was the theme, and He was near. But whatever is preached here fails; the people are the same—as hard as stones, and cold as ice. Not one stayed behind! O God, are these people judicially doomed? Oh, forbid it by Thy grace! Let me soon see that there is something to be done, even here. Give me more faith in Thee, and make me more faithful to Thee.

Nov. 18 (Sunday).—Preached three times, and had good meetings. O Lord, let not our services decline, but rather increase in power, that sinners may be saved. Oh, come nearer! I do long for the happy time when I shall see souls flocking to the Saviour in this place. That will be a rare sight to the angels of heaven.

Nov. 25 (Lord's Day). — Disconsolate all day— morning especially; never was I more cast down. O Lord, how long? Soon must I fail, unless Thou wilt smile upon me.

Dec. 2.—Often in the shade; much of last week was spent in gloomy regions. The Lord smiled a little upon me to-night—blessed be His name! How poor I am without Thee! How feeble and insipid my prayer and sermon! Oh, for the Spirit!

Dec. 5.—" Search me, O God, and know my heart; try me, and know my thoughts; and see if there be any wicked way in me, and lead me in the way everlasting." This was the prayer of the Psalmist. It shall be mine—I know it is mine! Oh, save me from self-deceit! How awful my inward corruption!

Dec. 6.—I read some of the biography of Jonathan Edwards. How cruelly treated at Northampton! What must be the spirit of those men, seeing they could cast out such a man into the cold world! Having been deprived of his support, he became so poor that he had no money to buy writing-paper: he had to write on old letters and on the margin of his books. How good ministers sometimes suffer! Give me something of the piety and pathos of Jonathan Edwards. Teach me Thy law, and lead me into all truth. When I stand to preach what I have prepared, oh, stand there by me! Help me to speak to men with plainness and great earnestness. Oh, let the message break my heart!

Dec. 14.—This afternoon I read some of the life of the seraphic Pearce. What a high degree of spirituality! I find that I am next to nothing; let my name be unmentioned. May I know something of that heart religion. During this year I sent the following to the *Tyst Apostolaidd :*—" The Reformation," p. 162; "The Bible," pp. 201, 226; Poetry, p. 141; Memoir of Ellis Evans, p. 169; "Jacob and his sons," p. 125; Psalm cx., p. 77.

1850. Jan. 2.—The year '49 has gone, and with it millions have passed to their graves! I am left. "How great Thy grace, O God, in sparing one so fruitless! My great want is to feel more of the importance of my work. I resolve to-night to pray more, and that more earnestly. Lord, aid me in that resolution."

Jan. 15.—To-day I finished my daily reading of the Old Testament, having begun it April 28th, 1848. During that time, also, I read the New Testament, and most of Barnes' notes. After that I read Beza's Latin Testament. I then commenced the Greek Testament, and have gone as far as the fourth gospel. During the same time I practised Pitman's Shorthand, and tran-scribed into it the whole of the New Selection Hymns; also read Hebrew and History of England.

Jan. 26.—Rather low for the last fortnight. It is no wonder, for I feel my heart so full of what I hate. O for a clean heart and a renewed spirit. But I must struggle on.

Jan. 27.—Sunday. Above the waves all day. The wind filled my sails and gave me much pleasure. " I bless Thee, my God."

Feb. 2.—My burden still is this sinful heart. O that I could hang the old tempter ! How is it that sin will not let me alone?

Feb. 3.—Sunday. Had a very happy day, an unusual help to preach. I hear that one has been wounded by the arrows, and is about to come into our midst. (Sent to the *Tyst Apostolaidd :*—" Luther," p. 59; " Hearing the Gospel," p. 79; " Abel Morgan and his Concordance," pp. 90, 111, 153, 234.)

## A Tour from Home.

Feb. 5.—Went to Blaenavon, got wet to the skin, but saved from cold. Preached at Horeb at seven o'clock: found some joy. Slept with my old friend Rev. Daniel Morgan. Spent Wednesday (6th) with him : a stormy day throughout. On Thursday (7th) I went to Blaenau (? Blaina), and preached in Mr. Roberts' Chapel: had much pleasure. Took supper with Mr. W. Hiley, and had much kindness there. Slept with Mr. Roberts, the minister; found " Nefydd " very kind. During the Friday I visited some old friends and acquaintances. At seven I preached at Tabor, Brynmawr. The Lord gave me much help. On Saturday I went to Sirhowy, getting very wet on the way, as it was stormy and snowing. I found refuge at the house of old Mrs. Williams, Penmark, where I had a change of clothes while my own were put to dry. May the Lord bless Mrs. Williams for her kindness to my unworthy self! Leaving Penmark, I went to Tredegar in company with Rev. Robert Ellis (Cynddelw), where we met "Cymro Bach," and had an interesting chat with him. From there I went to Rhymney, where I preached on the Sunday at Penuel Chapel: I lodged with my friend Mr. Isaac Price. Had a large congregation on Sunday, and good music, but I thought it would be very difficult to please so many people. However, I thought my great object should be to please God; and if I could do that, I would please His people. They gave me 15s. for my services—which I guessed was very liberal.

From Rhymney I returned to Sirhowy, and preached at Carmel on the Monday evening. The day was stormy and wet, but there was a good attendance. Slept at the house of Mr. Williams, the baker, where I had the greatest kindness. He and his wife are very religious.

Tuesday Morning.—I called to see Mr. Robert Ellis, and bought of him the "Cofiant" of Jones, Bridgend. I now began my way home. There was much snow—more than six inches deep—which made it troublesome to walk. Came to Brynmawr with some difficulty, and reached home safely in the evening. Was cheered to learn that some friends were recovering from a serious illness. Thus ended this journey. I had bad weather all the way, but much kindness everywhere. The Lord has preserved me through all the storms. May I love Him and serve Him better!

Feb. 14.—Last night I attended a meeting at the Cymreigyddion Hall, Abergavenny, where the expelled ministers—Everett, Dunn, and Griffith—were expected. The two latter attended, but the first-named was prevented by illness. There was much excitement in the town and district. At 7 p.m., Mr. John Daniel (a Baptist) took the chair, calling first on Mr. Dunn and then on Mr. Griffith to speak. Dunn is a most excellent, calm, and pathetic speaker. He rivetted the attention of the throng for three hours, and evoked much cheering. Then his colleague spoke for two hours. Afterwards, the opposite party was permitted to reply. Mr. John Wesley Thomas spoke for a long time, but it was a miserable speech, and he was often hissed. Dunn replied to all his objections in about twenty minutes, and to the satisfaction of the majority. The meeting passed two resolutions—condemnatory of the doings of the Wesleyan Conference with regard to the expelled, and of sympathy with the ministers so much wronged. The meeting broke up at 2 o'clock, having lasted seven hours! I was never at such a meeting before. May truth be victorious whoever has it.

Feb. 16.—Rather dull this week. Bad look-out for Sunday. We have just had a preparatory meeting. An old brother, who had not been to communion for six months, returned. May he have wisdom to behave better in future!

D

Feb. 17 (Sunday).—Nothing special. Rather void of effect; still, not entirely barren. Could not have expected it better.

Feb. 24 (Sunday).—Had much assistance to-day. Preached thrice.

Mar. 3 (Sunday).—Nothing very good to-day; rather dead, yet not entirely devoid of pleasure. Nearer, Lord!

Mar. 10 (Sunday).—Brother Benjamin Williams, Darrenfelen, preached here to-day. Had Welsh *Hwyl.* I preached at 2 and 6 in English. A good day. One young woman stayed with us. Lord, help her! May many follow, and the Lord get praise from hard Llanthewy.

Mar. 17 (Sunday).—Rather dead in the morning; better at night.

Mar. 24 (Sunday).—Preached three times (at Bryn gwenyn at 2.30), and the Lord gave me much light.

Mar. 31 (Sunday).—Preached twice; had much enjoyment.

April 6.—To-day I buried the first man I baptized— old Walter Jones. He was baptized on July 8th, 1849. He died at 80. His religious life was short, but there is reason to think he is saved.

April 7 (Sunday).—One of the best days I ever had. Preached three times. A promising young man (William Lewis) came on to-night. He is a son of Mr. Lewis, of Ffawydden, who is one of our deacons. That young man became one of the best members of the Church, and also a deacon. His good wife was the daughter of Mr. Williams, of " The Court," where

I lodged. They dwelt at " Tyhir," their own farm. W. Lewis died on Christmas Day, 1888, aged 60.

April 11.—At the funeral of one of our members (Mrs. Rachel Williams, Coedygelly) my text was from *Phil.* i. 21. She died testifying that she had found the Rock under her feet.

April 13.—We had a Society. Four came on for the first time, viz., Williams, Wernddu ; W. Williams, of " The Court," with Mary, his sister ; and John Jones, Pant. May they come in the right way. O my God, my heart is full of praise.

April 14 (Sunday).—Not so good as the previous Sunday. John Watkins, " Great House," came on : he is of the same family as those named before. Lord, bless him. He remained a faithful member (but in communion at Abergavenny, as he lived near there), and died in 1896.

April 23 (Tuesday night).—I was made miserable by toothache, could not sleep. Rose at 2 a.m., was at Abergavenny before 6, had it out, and am now in a new world.

May 12 (Sunday).—Good all day : hundreds were present, when I baptized 12 persons near Tresaeson. Everything passed well. Some said that I plunged them too deep, but I did not agree with them. Mr. Daniel Jones (the old minister of Llanthewy) preached twice in the Chapel. He had much sweetness about him. This day has cheered me much. *Laus Deo.* [Daniel Jones died July 11, 1850.]

May 19 (Sunday).—Preached at Penrose, having exchanged pulpits with old brother Cobner. The cause there is very low. On the Monday I went to Llanvihangel Crucorney tea party: preached in the evening with the Rev. Mr. Evans, of Tredegar. On Tuesday I went to Pontypool to the Annual Meetings of the College. I had the pleasure of hearing for the first time the Rev. Wm. Jones, of Cardiff. On Thursday I came home in joy and peace.

May 23.—Preached twice at Skenffrith. I had exchanged with Mr. Richards, the pastor: the cause is low.

May 26 (Sunday).—Preached twice: had much help. Two came on. May their motive be pure. I suspect one very much!

May 29 and 30.—The Association was held at "The Temple," Newport. Good Meetings; but only the 10 o'clock service was held in the open air, as heavy rain came on and we had to disperse to the chapels.

.      .      .      .      .      .

July 7.—Baptized six; all passed well, but the weather was bad. Mr. Jenkins, of Bradford College, came unexpectedly; he preached twice very eloquently. A hopeful young man.

July 14.—Preached three times. Good. Two came on.

July 21.—Insipid all day. I thought I had good sermons.

July 28.—Preached at Goitre. Mr. Edred Jones in my place. Went thence to Tredegar (Siloh) Quarterly Meeting. Poor meeting! No wonder, as there is much discord in the Church.

Aug. 4 (my Birthday).—Preached twice: had help. One came on.

Aug. 6.—I am now about to go to Cwmdwr to see my parents and old friends. Twelve months to this week I was there before. "Lord, be with me and keep me!" It is easy to preach when the Lord helps. On the 13th I returned; had a pleasant journey.

Aug. 18.—Preached twice, pretty fair. Margaret Yates came on: I doubt her motive. After a while she left; she had a young man in view who was a member. She saw that he had a partner and she turned away.

Aug. 29.—Walked down to Raglan: spent the afternoon with the pastor, Mr. Jones. Preached at his Chapel at 7 to a few people. What a heathen locality is this!

Sept. 1 (Lord's Day morning).—The weather is good. I have much work before me to-day: I have to baptize five, and to address the people four times. Do Thou help me! All the work has been done, yea well: a large congregation all day.

Sept. 10.—Went to Blaenavon to Havard's Ordination: preached at 7 p.m. Slept with Mr. Daniel Morgan. Wednesday morning walked to Abergavenny by 6.15 to meet Miss Williams and Miss Eunice Jones, Cwmera, whom I drove up to Llanwrtyd Wells. Had a pleasant drive. At night I slept at the house of Mr. Winston, my old master. On Thursday went to the Bont, thence to the Wells. The two young women and myself came down to Llangammarch, en route for home, arriving at Llanthewy Court by 8 p.m. I am thankful that we all arrived safe!

Sept. 29 (Communion Sunday).—Preached fairly in the morning. Mr. Knight, a Wesleyan brother, preached in the evening. I had gone to Llanelan to preach at Heolgeryg. Had a good meeting.

Oct. 3.—Twelve months to-day we held our thanksgiving for the harvest. It was then very wet; so it is at our thanksgiving to-day. Somehow, the prayers had "no go" in them.

There were good crops this year all over the country, and the weather was all we could wish: never a better harvest.

I preached at the evening meeting, and the rain had by that time ceased.

Oct. 8 and 9.—Attended a meeting for the re-opening of Pisgah: preached at 10, because others had failed to arrive. That was a disappointment; and the Rev. W. Thomas, the minister, was much cast down, because ministers who had promised to be there did not come. Heard Rev. D. R. Stephen in the evening, but he was not at his best. A grand day was expected, and but for that we had a grand failure.

Nov. 13.—Exchanged with Rev. Danl. Morgan, Blaenavon.

Nov. 13.—Attended a Tea at Llanfihangel Crucorney; preached in the evening with Mr. Jeavons, Longtown.

Nov. 14.—Preached at Mr. Watkins' Great House, a farm near Abergavenny. Mrs. Watkins is a member —her husband is not, but being ill we held a meeting there. Text was *Gal.* ii. 16.

Nov. 16.—In afternoon went to see a few poor and sick people; a sad condition: I feel I ought to be thankful.

Nov. 24 (Sunday).—Very wet and stormy, only about 30 in chapel, but I think the Lord was with us: no storms can stop Him.

Dec. 8.—Preached twice: very good all day. "Lord, make me more thankful. When I consider how sinful I am I wonder Thou dost give me help at all. Thy mercy is boundless."

Dec. 15.—Exchanged with Mr. Cobner. Day rather wet. Returned same evening, and reached home by 9 o'clock.

Christmas Day.—Delivered a lecture on "Luther and the Reformation," at the Chapel at 11 o'clock. Attended a Tea Party at Mozerah C.M. Chapel in the evening, in fine weather.

The Last Sabbath of the Year.—Preached thrice: in the morning at Frogmore Street, Abergavenny, Rev. Micah Thomas was present, and I felt timid; in the afternoon at Bryngwyn; and at home in the evening. Had much help all day. *Laus Deo.*

1851. Jan. 5.—Preached twice: good in the evening. [This year I preached several sermons on the Christian Church. The note I made at that time is this—"Religious discussion being now the great question, in consequence of the Pope's 'Bull,' and other matters, I thought it necessary to review our foundations, and to become thoroughly acquainted with the Christian Church as she is described in the New Testament." From 1852-1855, I preached a number of sermons on the *Book of Revelation.* I stopped at Chapter xii., owing to my change of abode. My object was, to acquaint myself with the meaning of that Book : being unwilling that any part of the Bible should be a blank to my mind. I read much and profited; but perhaps followed Barnes too much. —*Tyst Apostolaidd* 1851, p. 289 : a sermon on *Psa.* lxxiii. 24.]

Jan. 9.—Attended a lecture at the Cymreigyddion Hall at 7 p.m., on Astronomy, delivered by Rev. Micah Thomas. It was very comprehensive, eloquent, and lucid : the old man seemed quite at home with his theme.

Jan. 26.—Preached thrice : a miserable day—wet, cold and stormy. Few people, as a matter of consequence.

Feb. 2.—Mr. Knight preached for me. I preached at Caerphilly, from *Psa.* cxxxiii. and *Thess.* v. 17. A pleasant journey.

Feb. 12.—The Quarterly Meeting of the Eng. Baptists was held at our Chapel. Richards of Skenffrith, and Jones of Raglan preached the first evening. 13th at 10 : Dan Davies, Llanelly, and T. Thomas, Tutor. Afternoon : Lewis, Lanvapley, and Thomas, Mozerah (Indept. and Meth.) The Tutor in the evening. Good services, good attendance and fine weather.

March 4 and 5.—At the re-opening of Hermon, Nantyglo : Revs. Evans, Dowlais ; Thomas, Cefn ; Thomas the Tutor ; Hiley of Llanwenarth ; Jones of Zion, Merthyr ; "Cymro Bach" ; Jenkins of Hengoed ; and N. Thomas of Carmarthen, preached. Good meetings. I remember that B. Williams, of Darrenfelen, introduced one of the services by a powerful prayer :

he said, "Lord, we remember the opening of the first Hermon, and here is another opening: I am willing for the Church to have a new Chapel, but had they chosen a new God I would not have come near them."

[I kept a day school from 10th March to May 16th this year. There was no school in the parish, and I did it chiefly for the sake of poor children, who had their teaching almost for nothing. The parents, however, did not value their chance, sent their youngsters very irregularly, and so I closed the school. It was kept in the vestry, over the stable by the Chapel.]

May 21 and 22.—Attended the Annual Meetings of the College at Pontypool.

May 22.—We had an excellent Tea Party at our Chapel, and the day was fine. Speeches and singing in the evening.

May 25 (Sunday).—Good meeting in the morning. Visited Rachel Phillips of the Pentre in the afternoon. She is very ill, yet has much religion in her. She said, " I submit to His will, whether that be to restore or take me away. He knows what is best; I am not afraid of death, for Jesus is my friend." These were her words, and it was easy to pray in her chamber. Had a good meeting at 6; Sarah Lewis, Ffawydden, and Charlotte Redwood came before the Church: the first is hopeful.

May 27 and 28.—At the Association at Bethesda, Bassaleg.

June 1.—Preached twice. Mr. Jenkins of Bradford preached in the evening. Mary Morgan came on:

there is something very genuine about her; her mother is a member.

June 8.—Preached twice. Communion. Good all day; one young man—John Jones of Clytha—came on.

June 13.—Jane Phillips came on this (Friday) evening: a sister of Rachel Phillips. Their mother is a member.

June 17.—Went by the mail coach to Newport, thence by train to Cardiff. Preached at the Tabernacle with the Blind Man of Swansea. 18th, At the Association at Tongwynlais: preached in the evening with Mr. Price of Aberdare, at Melin Gruffydd. 20th, Went to see Llandaff Cathedral. In the evening I preached at Great House (Mr. Langley's), in the parish of Whitchurch. Went to Newport, thence to Holly House: had great kindness at Mr. Rees' hands. Preached twice at Bethel on Sunday, had much delight. On Monday went to Nantyglo: preached at Tabor, Brynmawr. On the 24th I reached home after a long and joyous journey.

June 26.—Warm day: at a tea party at Skenffrith.

June 30.—Rev. J. Jones, of Merthyr, preached here all day.

July 6 (Sunday).—Preached thrice; baptized six and received them. Miss Eunice Jones, of Cwmera, stayed with us in the evening: there are excellent signs about her, unless I am greatly mistaken.

July 20.—Had arranged to exchange with Rev. Francis Hiley: he did not come, owing to the death of his brother William the day previous. I went up in the morning and preached at Llanwenarth. Preached at Tudor Street at 3 p.m. Had 4/- for my service. Preached at home at 6 : good all day.

July 27.—Went over to Cwmera : at 10 o'clock I gave an address on Baptism by the river side, and immersed John, Eunice, and Mary, children of Mr. Jones, Cwmera. A crowd was present, and all passed off well. Mr. Morgan Lewis, Chapelyffin, preached at the house. I went to Bryngwenyn in the afternoon and preached. At home at 6 : had much help all day. Hard work and long walking. "Bless the Lord, O my soul!"

Aug. 3.—Preached twice : Communion. Received the three who were baptized at Cwmera. "May they hold on to the end!"

### A TOUR TO CWMDWR.

Aug. 5 (Tuesday).—Went to Brecon, and preached at Watergate. On Wednesday evening at Zoar, and on Thursday evening at Sardis. Went over the mountains to Cwmdwr on Friday : found my parents as well as I could expect. Preached at Horeb twice on Sunday. At Cefnarthen (Indpt. Chap.) Monday evening. At Horeb again on Tuesday evening. On Wednesday began my way home; turned to Llywel Churchyard, where some of my relatives on mother's side rest in peace. The following is on a small head-stone on grandparents' grave :—

THOS. EVANS of this parish : JOAN his wife.
She died May 26, 1820, ae. 70.
He died Jan. 17, 1821, ae. 81.

In the same grave lies the body of William Evans, their son, who was buried several years ago. He was the father of Rees Evans, who held pastorates at Neath, Liverpool, and in America. I knew Uncle William well : though an illiterate man he was very pious, and his death was happy. I reached home at Llanthewy on Thursday. *Laus Deo.* (See a memoir of Rees Evans, written by me in the *Greal* for 1885, p. 6.)

Aug. 17.—Preached twice ; two came on in the evening, for which I rejoice.

Aug. 24.—Preached twice at Skenffrith. Rev. J. Jones of Merthyr was at Llanthewy.

Aug. 25.—Attended the funeral of Miss Rachel Phillips, Pendre ; aged 17. She was very pious. I both baptized and buried her.

### To the Great Exhibition (London, 1851).

Sep. 15.—I and seven others from Llanthewy paid a visit to the great Metropolis, where we spent a week. Heard Baptist Noel, Hinton and Brock. By economy I spent 3 guineas only. Returned safely on the 23rd. I cannot attempt to describe the journey.

Sep. 28.—Preached thrice. Communion. Baptized three in the morning.

Oct. 1 (Wednesday).—Had our Harvest Thanksgiving—three services. Fair meetings ; preached at 6 o'clock. Wet all day.

### A Collecting Tour to Bristol.

Oct. 14 (Tuesday).—Went to Abergavenny ; thence to Pontypool. Left there on Wednesday morning at 5 ; had it rough to cross the Channel : at Bristol before 10 : took lodging at Rev. Thos. Jenkins' house, which suited me nicely. Wednesday afternoon called on a few Pontypool College Subscribers. Visited the College: a large library; many old and rare books, especially Bibles of the 16th and 17th centuries. Saw a small but valuable original portrait of Oliver Cromwell. Saw John Bunyan's Concordance, small and much worn. Saw Tyndale's Testament, printed at Antwerp in 1526, the only perfect copy in the world; it is in good condition and beautiful. From this Bagster printed his copy. Saw Rev. Josh. Thomas' MSS., two small 4to vols. written in a small, fine hand. Called on the President, Mr. Crisp, a very friendly old gentleman, thin, pale and quiet. Thursday and Friday at 8 o'clock heard Mr. Vincent lecture at the Broadmead Rooms. Altho' I did not feel well on the Friday I went out: found it difficult to meet the Subscribers, some of whom I had to call on several times. On Sunday I preached at 10 in Mr. Jenkins' Chapel. Heard Mr. Crisp in Broadmead Chapel in the afternoon. Preached for Mr. Probert at the Pithay at 6: after that I hurried to Broadmead. and heard most of Mr. Haycroft's Sermon. Too much style there! On each side of the Broadmead pulpit there are marble tablets, from which I copied the following :—

In Memory of
The Rev. BARNARD FOSKETT,
Pastor of this Church 34 years,
Died Sep. 17th, 1758, aged 73.

———

In Memory of
The Rev. JOHN RYLAND, D.D.
Pastor of this Church 31 years,
Died May 25th, 1825, ae. 72.

———

The Rev. HUGH EVANS, A.M.
Pastor of this Church 23 years,
Died March 28th, 1781, ae. 64.

———

The Rev. ROBT. HALL, A.M.
Pastor of this Church 5 years,
Died 21st Feb., 1831, ae. 66.

———

The Rev. CALEB EVANS, D.D. Pastor of this Church 10 years, Died Aug. 9th, 1791, ae. 54.

The Rev. SAMUEL SUMMERS, Pastor of this Church 3 years, Died 15th Dec., 1836, ae. 46.

The Righteous shall be in everlasting remembrance.

The Memory of the Just is Blessed.

I left Bristol on Thursday 4.30 p.m. per steamer, and reached Pontypool by 9.30. Returned to Llanthewy by noon on Friday.

Oct. 26.—Preached twice. Communion: rather flat.

Nov. 6.—At the funeral of old John Stephens, Coedmorgan, aged 76. He was buried near our Chapel. He had been a hearer of the Gospel for more than 50 years, yet had not confessed Christ! Went to Cwmera and preached at 7 o'clock.

Nov. 7.—At a tea party at Llanfihangel Crucorney. Mr. Morgan Lewis and I preached in the evening.

Nov. 30.—Preached twice at Nazareth, Clydach. Communion.

Dec. 4.—Thursday evening, preached at Cwmera.

Dec. 7.—Preached twice in English: Williams, Darrenfelen, twice in Welsh. Fine day. Good meetings. Williams collected £1 15s. towards his Chapel debt.

Dec. 11.—Went to the Cefn, a farm-house about six miles away, where I preached; returning in a dry moonlight night, in the company of my constant friend, Mr. Williams, "The Court," with whom I lodged for 4 years. He was a deacon and our precentor, and a better friend to a minister seldom could be found. He died at a good old age.

Dec. 14.—Preached twice at Penrose. Cause very low.

Dec. 18.—Officiated at the Marriage of Thos. Williams, Tresaeson, and Rebecca Lewis, of Ffawydden: they were the first ever married at this Chapel. Mr. Ellis, Registrar, was present.

Dec. 21.—Communion Sunday: very wet. Baptized one in the flood.

Christmas Day: gave a lecture in our Chapel on "The sufferings of the Baptists in England, etc.," which passed off well.

(The substance of this lecture was translated by me into Welsh, and it appeared in the *Seren Gomer*, 1852, pp. 173, 215, 414.)

Last Sabbath of '51.—Preached thrice. Had much help all day.

1852. Jan. 1.—Preached at Cwmera.

Jan. 18 (Sunday).—Preached twice. Communion. I felt rather "undewy:" the congregation of late is thinner; some gone away, some careless, several ill. "Do Thou not leave us, O God of our Salvation!"

Jan. 28.—Went to Coedgelly to see old Mrs. Jones, who has been ill for a while. Found her more happy in mind than usual. She said, "I have done here, I want to go. *There* is my home, *there* I want to be, *there* is my all: plenty there for the whole family. O! to go, come quickly Lord, O come!" Such were some of her words. I was much impressed with the value of religion when at her bedside: had unusual pathos in prayer.

Jan. 29.—Mr. Williams and I went to Cwmera. Rather wet; preached there; many present; good meeting. We had a happy time; a pleasant moonlight walk, and home before midnight.

Feb. 4.—Buried old Mrs. Jones, Coedgelly, who died Jan. 30, aged 76; our oldest member, she having been a communicant 50 years. Large funeral; I spoke from *John* v. 28, 29.

Feb. 16.—Went to Caerphilly to see my chosen one, Miss Fox. Had solid talk with Mrs. Edmunds.

Feb. 29 (Sunday).—Preached twice at Penrose; a student in my place.

March 28.—Exchanged pulpits with Mr. Williams, Darrenfelen. Mr. Knight preached with him in English in the evening.

April 1.—Left "The Court," where I had spent a happy four years and three months. The family were extremely kind. The same evening I baptized two young women at Frogmore Street, after an able discourse on "Baptism" by Rev. Micah Thomas, the pastor. Slept at his house that night.

April 2 (Friday).—I was married to Miriam Fox, who had spent half of her life with her uncle and aunt (Mr. and Mrs. Edmunds) at Caerphilly. The wedding took place at Frogmore Street Chapel, Abergavenny. I regarded it an honour to be married by the good old tutor. The weather was delightful. We stayed in town most of the day, at the house of my wife's parents, returning in the evening to our cottage at Llanthewy. Friends welcomed us on the way and at the house. Lord, bless our union, and help us to walk in Thy fear. Amen. [Prayer answered.] My wife was baptized at Caerphilly in 1842. This

note was written by her in a small pocket-book:—
"Feb. 6, 1842: I have this day publicly professed my attachment to the Redeemer by following Him in the ordinance of Baptism. Oh, that I may be enabled, by the assistance of the Holy Spirit, to endure unto the end!" Her prayer was answered.

April 4.—Preached thrice at home; very good all day. My wife and I went to dine at "The Court."

April 11.—Communion; "Cymro Bach" preached for me, and collected for our missions.

April 25.—Preached twice at Penrose; a student in my place.

April 30.—To-day we have beautiful and much-needed rain. It has been very dry since February; vegetation very backward; wheat, however, looks well.

May 6.—I married John Roberts and Mary Dobbs, of Abergavenny, at our chapel.

May 27.—A fine day. At a tea meeting at Penrose.

May 31.—At a tea meeting at Llanfihangel Crucorney.

June 2.—At the funeral of old John Prosser, aged 82; he could read with spectacles to the end. I spoke from *Ps.* xxiii. 1-4.

Aug. 7.—Went to Caerphilly to see my wife; had several showers on the way. On Sunday preached at Tonyfelin twice; Rev. O. Williams, Treforest, with me, as I had not sent a publication. Stayed with Mrs. Edmunds at Caerphilly until Wednesday morning. Had it very wet to return; arrived at our cottage by 8 p.m. The weather is bad, and the fields

E

want harvesting; much damage already done. May the Lord have pity on our land, and that speedily!

Aug. 15.—Preached twice at Penrose; rather flat all day.

Aug. 22.—Preached twice at Frogmore Street; Rev. Micah Thomas had gone to Swansea. Ordinance Sunday; had much freedom.

Sept. 1 (Wednesday evening).—Attended a mission meeting at Lion Street Chapel, Abergavenny. Mr. Brown, of Reading, and Mr. Wheeler, a missionary from Africa, were present; a very effective meeting.

Sept. 27.—Spoke at the funeral of Elizabeth Morgan, a member whom I baptized last year; aged 54. She was a good woman; suffered greatly from cancer in her breast. All pain is now over!

Sept. 29.—Married John Watkins, Great House, to Sarah James, Penlanlau, at our chapel. I baptized John some time ago.

Oct. 3.—Preached twice. I was as " dry " as the season!

Oct. 6 (Wednesday).—Our thanksgiving meeting for harvest. Preached at six from *Hosea* iv. 1: " For the Lord hath a controversy," etc. Did not write any of my sermon.

Oct. 13.—Went to Cwmdwr to see my parents; returned Friday.

Dec. 5.—Preached thrice. It has been wet for five or six weeks.

Dec. 12 (Sunday).—We are generally careful to deck our persons before we go to the Lord's house: we ought to be more concerned about inward fitness for worship—be prepared to appear before men and God. Preached twice.

Dec. 19.—This is the seventh wet Sunday. Preached twice, fairly.

Dec. 25 (Christmas).—Delivered a discourse on " Christmas " at eleven. Showery afternoon. At the funeral of Mrs. James, of the Fâs; aged 63. After that I went to Mozerah tea-party, and returned by 9 p.m.

Dec. 26.—Preached twice. An awful storm at night. We shall hear of losses.

Dec. 28.—Wife and I visited Mr. Charles Davies, Pontypool, returning on Friday. Heard to-day of the very sudden death of poor father. He died on the 22nd of this month, out on the road—it was supposed in a fit. How I feel after him!

**1853.** Jan. 9.—Wet weather still continues. Mr. E. H. Davies, of Pontypool (my wife's cousin), preached for me in the evening.

Jan. 16.—Preached twice. Still wet—serious time!

Jan. 23.—Preached twice; collected for the Irish Mission. This is the first fine Sunday for fourteen weeks!

Jan. 27 (Thursday).—My wife gave birth to our first child—a boy. All is well, and I am thankful to our God. If the little one entrusted to us shall live, may he be a Christian in deed! More we cannot desire for him, and less will not do. His name shall be Thomas Harris Lewis. The good old Harrises of Blaenau and Llanwenarth were my wife's ancestors, (See an account of them in *Seren Cymru* for Aug. 21, 1863; and *Seren Gomer*, 1864, p. 19.)

April 26 (Tuesday).—Began my journey to Cwmdwr; halted at Llangynider. On Wednesday went to Llangorse and saw a few old friends. Visited that awful place in the village of Llanfihangel-tal-y-llyn where a house was burnt down some time ago, and eight persons perished; only the head of the family escaped —a wretched man and a drunkard. The ruin had a ghastly appearance.

Arrived in Brecon at 3 o'clock; saw my sister Margaret. Preached at Watergate at 7 o'clock; had a long chat with Mr. Edwards, the pastor.

Thursday morning, began my way to Llanfihangel. Saw my dear old pastor, Rev. Thos. Williams, and his wife. Had a short conversation with him: he was just leaving home. Preached at 7.30 at Zoar; many present. Slept at Fasygerwn.

Friday morning, very wet; but I must go to Cwmdwr. I was saved from wetting; saw a few old friends; preached there at 3 p.m. Found my mother better than she had been; most of her time in bed; cannot sleep at night. She is resigned and contented, and often sings as well as her asthma will allow. In the night I heard her sing :—

"O na allwn garu'r Iesu, yn fwy ffyddlon a'i wasnaethu,
    Dweyd yn dda mewn gair am dano, a rhoi fy hun yn gwbl iddo."

"O that I with holy fervour, loved and served my blessed Saviour;
    In each act spoke of Him sweetly; gave myself to Him completely."

May 1 (Sunday).—Preached thrice at Cwmdwr: morning and evening at Horeb; in the afternoon at mother's house, as she had not heard a sermon for some time. Never did I preach with more freedom. Had a large attendance all day.

May 2.—Rose early, and went to see old friends; found some bedridden through old age. Saw old Thomas Williams, the quarryman, a faithful Christian for 60 years; now not able to leave his bed much. It is strange to see his old place at Horeb empty, as he was always there. I read, prayed, and talked with him. He said he was very happy: that it was heaven often with him on his bed of affliction. He died soon after my visit. I bid adieu to many old faces that I shall never again see on earth.

Mother was very low when I left her, and so was I. I looked hard at her when going out, fully believing that I shall never again see her alive.

Having walked to Trecastle, I took the coach to Brecon. Slept at the house of Mr. T. Thomas, Llanvase: very kind people.

Tuesday morning rather wet. Rev. D. B. Edwards accompanied me for about three miles. Called at Elormeirch; saw Mr. Cadwgan Edwards and family, from whom I had the greatest kindness. (They were a family from Cwmdwr, and had lived at a farm called Clynfoel.) Was with Rev. R. Johns by tea-time; preached at his chapel at seven, and afterwards slept at his house.

Wednesday morning Mr. Johns and I went to Brecon. I took the mail at 3 p.m., and was at Llanthewy by night. Found all well. *Laus Deo.*

When at Cwmdwr I went to Llandovery and over to Llanfair-ar-y-bryn Church, where I saw the tomb of

the great hymnist, W. Williams of Pantycelyn. Why
he is buried behind the Church I know not. This is
the inscription on the stone :—

Sacred
To the Memory of
The Late Reverend WILLIAM WILLIAMS, of Pantycelyn
in this Parish,
Author of several works in prose and verse.
He waits here the coming of the Morning Star,
Which shall usher in the Glories of the first Resurrection,
When at the sound of the Archangel's trump
The sleeping dust shall be reanimated,
And death for ever shall be swallowed up in victory.
He laboured in the service of the Gospel for near half a century, and
continued incessantly to promote it, both by
His labours and writings :
And to his inexpressible joy beheld its influence extending,
And its efficacy witnessed in the conviction and conversion
of many thousands.
After languishing some time, he finished his course and life together
January 11th, 1791 : aged 74.
Heb saeth, heb fraw, heb ofn, heb ofid, ac heb boen ;
Yn canu o flaen yr orsedd, Ogoniant pur yr Oen ;
Ynghanol Myrdd Myrddiynau, yn caru oll heb drai,
Yr Anthem ydyw Cariad, a chariad i barhau.

Also of the Remains of
MARY,
The pious and beloved wife of the said
William Williams,
Who departed this life the 11th of June, 1799 : aged 76.
Her unfeigned Piety, amiable conduct, and unblameable Deportment
through life are too well known to
require any further
Encomium.

Near the tomb of William Williams is the monument to his son, on which is the following in large capital letters :—

Sacred
To the Memory of the
Reverend JOHN WILLIAMS,
Pantycelyn, in this Parish.
In whom Learning, Piety and Benevolence were united.
He devoted a considerable part of his wealth to the transmission of the
Glorious Gospel to all lands.
He died June the 5th, 1828 : aged 74 years.
Stranger, shouldst thou approach this awful shrine,
The merits of the honoured dead to seek ;
The Friend, the Son, the Christian, the Divine,
Let those who knew him, those who loved him, speak.
A Sinner Saved.

The last line was inserted at the request of the deceased.

May 8.—Communion : Preached two old sermons; was rather flat—a dry day in more than one sense. It is very cold for the time of the year—and snowing !

May 18 and 19.—At the Annual Meetings of the Pontypool College : heard Revs. E. Evans, Dowlais, and J. Jordan Davies preach. Texts : 1 *Tim.* iv. 6, 7 ; *Col.* i. 26, 27.

May 22 (Sunday).—Preached thrice at Raglan ; walked 20 miles during the day; reached home late. Very happy services.

May 29.—Preached twice ; never under greater disadvantage. Had severe cold, hoarseness, and toothache. My voice nearly gone, but it improved before the end of the evening service. Very ill during the night, and in great pain.

June 23.—Rev. John Jones, of Merthyr, preached at our Chapel two sermons of 25 minutes each (one in English, *Ps.* i. 1-3; and the other in Welsh, *John* ix. 27). Good attendance, but the English sermon was flat, while the Welsh was good.

July 3.—Communion Service: I had, alas! to expel a young woman named Sarah Davies, whom I baptized July 7, 1850.

July 9.—Went to Abergavenny, and married at Frogmore Street (as deputy for Mr. Thomas, who was at Swansea) one Harrison to Elizabeth Rosser.

July 10.—Preached twice; a fine day in the midst of wet. Harvest has come, but the season is unfavourable. Lord, pity the unworthy!

July 16th.—Have just read in the *Hereford Times* a full account of the tremendous floods of the 8th and 9th instant. Many houses have been swept away; one, near Builth, with five persons, all perished. In other places persons were drowned also. The flood was terrific at Brecon Town. Much property was lost; bridges have been demolished; cattle and hay have been swept away. The floods of last year and this will not be soon forgotten.

July 18.—Last Tuesday preached at the funeral of a young wife named Sarah Brewer, aged 28. Wet weather still continues—it is alarming!

July 24.—Preached twice at Frogmore Street for Mr. Thomas. I had a desire to preach on a certain text, but in the pulpit a thought rushed upon me that he is the greatest sinner on earth who thinks of exalting himself where Christ only should be exalted; and my conceit soon gave way.

July 26 and 27.—At our quarterly meeting at Horeb, Blaenavon. Good all through. Rev. James Rowe's sermon on *Gen.* vii. 16, "And the Lord shut him in," was excellent, and made a very deep impression. The preacher dwelt upon the character and safety of Noah. The other preachers were: Revs. D. Ll. Isaac; Richards, Carnarvon; Morgan, Bridgend (Eng.); Tim. Thomas; Thomas Thomas (the Tutor, Eng.); Thomas Evans, Pontypool; Price, of Abersychan (Eng.); W. Thomas, Pisgah; Dan. Davies, Llanelly; D. Edwards, Temple, Newport; and myself (Eng.).

Aug. 7.—Preached twice at Nebo, Ebbw Vale; good meetings. The weather is now fine, and harvest is progressing. *Laus Deo.*

Aug. 14.—Preached twice. Beautiful weather. This week we held prayer meetings for a revival among us. We had five meetings, the last on Sunday, Aug. 21, May good follow.

Sept. 28.—Went to Caerphilly to fetch my wife and boy; borrowed car of Mr. Williams, The Court. Had some rain.

Oct. 2.—Went to Goitre. Communion; preached twice. The cause is very low, and so it might be, as there is no union and order.

Oct. 13.—Miss Mary Davies, of Pontypool (my wife's cousin), concluded her visit to us. She was the daughter of Mr. Charles Davies, ironmonger, of that town. Miss Davies was one of the most amiable and pious young women I ever knew. To spend an hour in her society was to be lifted up from earth to heaven. Her education and accomplishments were dedicated to the service of the Lord. She died at Abergavenny in March, 1873, aged 35.

Oct. 19.—We held our Thanksgiving meetings for harvest; it was wet and cold. Preached in the evening from *Ps.* c. 4. The harvest this year is bad, about half the average; wheat and barley out even now; spring wheat better than expected.

Oct. 30.—Old Mr. Kinsey (one of the first students at Abergavenny in 1807) preached in Welsh in the morning, and I preached twice in English.

Nov. 17.—Preached in the evening at Cefncoch, at Mr. Webb's house; many present.

Nov. 20.—Alas! we had to expel—temporarily— John Williams, The Court, and his wife; but fortunately they were restored without much noise or delay.

Nov. 29.—Have just heard of the sudden death of the Rev. Micah Thomas, which took place at seven o'clock last night. This day week I was with him for a long time, as usual on Tuesdays.

Dec. 5 (Monday).—A fine day. At the funeral of Rev. Micah Thomas; hundreds present besides those who were invited. There was deep sorrow depicted on many faces. Mr. Clark, of Monmouth, read and prayed in the Chapel; Dr. Thomas (the Tutor) delivered an appropriate address; and Mr. Thomas Jones, of Chepstow, spoke at the grave. The old Vicar, Rev. W. Powell, was present.

Dec. 20.—Went up to Brecon; the next day I reached Cwmdwr. Mother had been buried the day before.

Her death was not to be lamented, as she had suffered much from dropsy and asthma. During the next three days I visited many old friends. On Sunday I preached at Horeb. Communion there; our meetings were sweet. On Sunday afternoon had a long talk with an old woman of 85, who had been in her youth a hearer of the eminent Daniel Rowland, of Llangeitho. All she told me I had read of that noted preacher. Monday morning, at seven, I started homeward on horseback.

**1854.** Jan 1.—Heavy snow. Preached twice; small attendance.

Jan. 4.—Failed to hold the Wednesday Prayer Meeting, as the snow had filled the road, in some places to the top of the hedges. *Note.*—I went, but found the Chapel locked; not one there except myself.

Jan. 31.—For the past six months I have acted as nurse as well as pastor. Our baby will not sleep except on my lap; during this time I have read volumes—"History of the Calv. Methodists," "Methodistiaeth Cymru," and other works.

Feb. 2.—Preached in the evening at Cefncoch.

Feb. 5 (Sunday).—Preached twice at Lion Street Chapel; cause low.

Feb. 14.—Went to Caerphilly, returning next day.

March 2.— Preached at Cefncoch; had much help.

April 17.—Attended a tea party at Raglan.

April 23.—Preached twice at Pontrhydyrun, having exchanged with Rev. D. D. Evans. Fine chapel; small attendance.

April 26.—This day is ordered by our Government for humiliation and prayer before God, that He may favour our arms in the present war between Russia and Turkey. We did not keep this day because commanded, but because it was convenient. In the evening I gave an address suitable to the times.

May 7.—Communion. Baptized James of Ffawydden and Edward Williams; restored Jonathan Davies.

May 11.—Buried James Redwood, Penypark, aged 65. Went to Penrose tea meeting; returned same evening.

May 16.—Married James Price (late of Ffawydden) and Mary Prosser (late of Church Farm) at our Chapel; both are members.

May 23 and 24.—At the Annual Meetings of the Pontypool College, Revs. Timothy Thomas and S. Price, Abersychan, preached.

May 25.—Our Tea Party for the Sunday School; goodly number present. As the people are on their way home rain coming down in torrents. Their fine dresses will be washed out, but their *pride* will not be.

May 30.—At Castleton Association; a large gathering. On the Wednesday I had to return to bury Isaac Edwards, aged 37, at our place. Spoke from *Heb.* ix. 27. He had been an invalid for more than four years. He was not a member.

June 18.—Preached twice. Am alone, my family having gone to visit Mrs. Edmunds, at Caerphilly. Dined at my old home—The Court. What a kind man I have ever found Mr. Williams.

June 25.—Preached at Goitre in the morning, and at home in the evening. After this meeting we had a short society, and one of the deacons (Mr. Lewis, of Ffawydden) stood up and said, "We want you to attend, in particular, Wednesday evening, as we have something of importance, and I may as well tell you it is about Mr. Lewis's salary. He is unsatisfied with what he has, and says he can't make a comfortable living of it" (£37 a year!). How clumsy and abrupt! I was much struck with its uncouthness. May the Lord's will be done also in this matter! If it be His will, I am willing to go to some other place; and I am willing to remain at Llanthewy. Lord, be with me!

June 30.—At the funeral of Rev. Benj. Price (Cymro Bach). He died at Bristol, where he had been for some time. The body was brought by train from Newport at 1.10. At Abergavenny Station upwards of twenty ministers and forty other friends met the train, and a procession was thus formed: The hearse, then about seven vehicles, men on horseback and on foot, composed of ministers in twos. At Llanwenarth Mr. Hiley preached very pathetically from *Acts* xx. 24. Rev. T. Jenkins, of Bristol (at whose house the late Benj. Price expired), read and prayed. Mr. Price was laid in the family grave, close to the wall of the Chapel. We have lost thus one of the most useful and universally-respected Baptist ministers in the Principality. His age was 62. A popular and witty preacher, a great writer in our Welsh magazines, an amiable friend and companion, a Christian of un-blemished character. He was very widely known, and his death will be felt throughout Wales, and in the Mission House in London.

July 9.—Preached thrice at Raglan; small congregations, but better at Kincoed, the outlying station.

July 16.—Preached twice at Lion Street Chapel, and at three o'clock in the old Welsh Chapel, Tudor Street. Mr. Hiley was present, but compelled me to stand in his place. He feels old age, and he is glad to be spared.

July 17.—At the funeral of little Tom Williams, of Bryncam, aged four years and three months. He fell into a pool by the house and was drowned. He was buried in his mother's grave, who died at his birth. It was pathetic to see him laid on her blackened coffin !

July 23.—Preached twice at Penrose. I want to feel the Spirit more!

Aug. 8 and 9.—At our Quarterly Meeting at Ebenezer, Blaenavon; good all through. I preached in English in the afternoon.

Oct. 1.—Exchanged with Mr. Hiley, of Llanwenarth. Preached thrice. Copied the following from the gravestone of one of the old ministers. The stone is at the back of the Chapel. On the upper part of the stone is the verse beginning, " Here lieth one of Abel's race," etc. (*vide* Josh. Thomas, Bap. Hist., p. 186). Then follow: "Joshua James, of y$^e$ Towne of Bergavenny; died August 22nd, 1728, aged 63. Here also lyeth the body of Elizabeth, y$^e$ wife of Joshua James, who deceased Feby. 15th, 1729, aged 42." Rev. James Lewis is interred, as it is supposed, in their grave. So said Mr. F. Hiley.

Oct. 3.—Held our Thanksgiving Meeting ; fine day, and good attendance. Preached at six from *Ps.* c. 4, 5. We never had a better harvest for the corn ; hay harvest fickle. Surely we have had ample reason for praise this year.

Oct. 8 (Sunday).—Exchanged with Rev. B. Williams, Darrenfelen. On Monday evening preached at Bethlehem, Llanelly (Brec.). On Tuesday went with Mr. Dan. Davies to Crickhowell to the annual meeting there. Preached in English. Mr. Francis Hiley followed in Welsh. Home on Thursday—all well. *Laus Deo.*

Oct. 22.—Communion ; fine day. Expelled Charlotte Redwood. I never knew a more worthless person. Had no opinion of her when she was baptized.

Oct. 23.—At Pontypool. Slept at the house of Mr. Charles Davies, Ironmonger. Mr. Thomas Evans, Tabernacle, and myself went together on Tuesday morning to the Quarterly Meeting at Old Blaenau. Preached the first evening with Robert Ellis, Cynddelw, and Evan Thomas, Tredegar. Two deacons were appointed at ten. Revs. Jas. Davies, Tabor ; W. Thomas, Pisgah ; and Thomas, Newport, officiated. At the other meetings, Revs. Dl. Morgan, Blaenavon ; Timothy Thomas ; Evans, Pontypool ; Dan. Davies, and Theophilus Jones, America, preached. Arrived home Thursday. On my journey I had a talk with Rev. Mr. Fuller, of Cardiff, and his son, who is in Bristol College.

Nov. 5.—Preached twice at Crickhowell. Communion.

Nov. 27.—At the funeral of old Mrs. Williams, Tresaeson. She was our senior member. Baptized 47 years ago at Llanwenarth. She was 78 years of age. I spoke from *Job* v. 26. A silent member; did not murmur in her affliction, but often said:

'Iesu anwyl, derbyn fi, Dere, cymer fy enaid atat ti dy hun."

Dec. 4.—Went to collect for Penrose. On Monday evening preached at Tabernacle, Pontypool. Tuesday morning, went to Pontrhydyrun, and spent a few hours with Rev. D. D. Evans; thence to Ponthir, and preached at seven. Wednesday, called at Caerleon; thence to Newport, and preached at Charles Street, subsequently making several calls. In the afternoon went to Cardiff, and preached at the Tabernacle. All there were in mourning after Rev. David Jones. I slept at the house of old Evan Llewellyn. Had a few hours with Sam. Evans (Gomer). On Friday went to Caerphilly, and sojourned with Mrs. Edmunds. Saturday morning, walked to Pontypool, and home by train; had a very comfortable journey, and collected a few pounds.

Dec. 10.—Preached at Penrose; hard, frosty weather.

Dec. 14.—Preached at Mr. Webb's, Cefncoch: good service.

Dec. 17.—Communion; baptized Mary Ann Edwards, Gardener's Hall.

Dec. 20.—Blaenavon; preached at Horeb. Thursday, at Varteg; dined with Mr. Isaac Hiley; preached at Pisgah. Friday, to Pontypool; walked to Beulah, and preached there. Saturday, walked to Maesycwmmer; preached on Sunday at Hengoed; the old church is rather low. Returned home on Christmas Day. The following I copied at Hengoed:—"In memory of pious Thomas Davies, of Llandinam, in the County of Montgomery, Minister of the Gospel, who died Apl. yᵉ 11th, 1756, aged 59 years." This stone has been put as a step into the chapel—too bad! (*Vide* "Jos. Thomas," p. 118.)

Dec. 31.—Preached twice; had much liberty. This year has been rather barren to Zion. Oh, for better times! Amen.

**1855.**—Preached twice on this first Sunday; had much joy.

Jan. 23.—Purchased ten copies of Mr. McPhun's Bible, for which I paid him ten guineas; by this means I received a free copy for myself. The Bibles gave satisfaction.

Jan. 24.—Preached at Llanwenarth; all passed fairly well.

Jan. 29.—Married Mr. John Morgan, Govilon, to Miss Sarah Lions, of Ffawydden. [She died in a few years.] After the wedding I went to Newport, and walked to Cefn, where I preached. Tuesday, walked with Mr. Tim. Thomas to Twyngwyn. Mr. Rowe was with us. Had a good quarterly meeting. Wednesday night, preached at Beulah; slept at the house of Mr. Llewellyn Jenkins (son of Dr. Jenkins, of Hengoed). Reached home on Thursday. *Laus Deo.*

Feb. 11.—Roads full of snow; few at Communion.

Feb. 14.—Rev. Robert Ellis (Cynddelw) preached at our chapel.

F

Feb. 18.—Preached twice at Pisgah, and collected. Mr. W. Thomas preached at Llanthewy. On Monday evening I visited Mr. Chas. Conway at Pontnewydd. He was very kind: gave me a sovereign. Preached at Pontrhydyrun; spent a few hours with Rev. Mr. Evans. Reached home next day.

Feb. 25.—Preached at Pontypridd; Communion; did not please myself. Had much talk with Rev. Jas. Richards; liked him very much. Returned on Monday through Cardiff. The great frost of six weeks breaks up; many people have wanted food.

March 22.—Married Jas. Jones, Tydraw, to Miss Ann Knight, "The Helms"; stormy and snowy day.

April 3.—Married John Turner, a smith from Llanover, to Mary Hopkins, a farmer's daughter from Llanfair.

April 15.—Preached twice. We got up a petition to Parliament in favour of Sir W. Clay's Bill for Entire Abolition of Church Rates.

April 25 and 26.—The quarterly meeting was held here. Preachers: Revs. Roberts, of Bethel; James, Beulah; Thomas, the Tutor; F. Hiley; Roberts, of Trosnant; Griffiths, Ponthir; Morgan, Blaenavon; J. Lewis, Usk; and Robert Ellis, Cynddelw. We had very good meetings.

May 17 (Thursday).—At 4 a.m. my second boy was born; both mother and child are doing well. His name shall be Caleb James, in memory of Rev. James Edmunds, of Caerphilly (my wife's uncle), and of Caleb his son, who died when a student at Bristol

College. May the Lord give grace to the lad, and be his God for ever. Amen.

May 26.—Married Mr. Wm. Lewis, of Ffawydden, to Miss Sarah Williams, of the Church Farm, at our chapel. May the Lord bless them : they are both faithful members.

May 27.—Preached thrice; had wonderful help all through the day, but I nearly spoiled all by being too long!

June 7.—Married John Williams, Little Mill, near Abergavenny, to Martha Powell, daughter of our chapel keeper.

June 18.—Went to Dowlais, and thence to Aberdare Association; very large congregations, and fine weather. I preached with Rev. T. Davies, of High Street, Merthyr, in the English Baptist Chapel. I felt very timid, and, strange to say, Mr. Davies said he felt the same.

July 8.—Preached thrice: at Llanwenarth morning and evening ; at Tudor Street at three.

July 22.—Preached twice at Zion, Pontypool : very good day.

July 24 and 25.—At Llanwenarth Quarterly Meeting. Great power attended some of the sermons. I preached in English in the afternoon—flat !

Aug. 17.—Went to Caerphilly for my family ; returned in the evening.

Aug. 19.—Preached twice at Raglan, and once at Kincoed.

Aug. 25.—Went to Llanvapley, to the Independent Chapel, to bury an old man named Wm. Edmunds, aged 75, the minister being ill.

Sept. 10.—We have had no rain of late; noble harvest. *Laus Deo.*

Sept. 28.—A journey from home to look for another church. On Friday preached at Beulah; Sunday, at Pontypridd; Monday, at Treforest; Tuesday, at Cowbridge; Wednesday, at Aberafan; Thursday, at Bethesda, Swansea; Friday, at Priory Street, Carmarthen.

Oct. 7 (Sunday).—Preached at Cowbridge; Monday, at Bridgend; Tuesday, at Cadoxton Monthly Meeting; Wednesday, at Pontypridd; Thursday till Saturday, at Caerphilly with Mrs. Edmunds.

Oct. 14 (Sunday).—At Docks, Cardiff. A comfortable journey, and had many good meetings. *Laus Deo.*

Nov. 3.—Went to Pontypridd. Preached on Sunday: a good day. Monday, preached at Salem, Cymmer: good. Tuesday, preached at Dinas, and had *hwyl*. Wednesday, went to Llantrissant Quarterly Meeting. I preached at two on Thursday, preceding Mr. Jones, of Zion. Reached home same day—thanks for the railway.

Nov. 25.—Preached thrice at Pontypridd, and baptized two in the afternoon. They talk of giving me a call, but I do not like some things there.

Dec. 21.—Went to Cefnmawr (North Wales); slept at night with my old fellow-student, E. Roberts, Cefnbychan. Had some hours with Rev. Ellis Evans. On Saturday went to Wrexham; and on Sunday preached twice in English. On Christmas Day, at eleven, preached in the same place. At their tea meeting in the afternoon. Thursday, went to Cefnmawr, and preached at Ellis Evans' chapel. Stayed with him at night; his whole talk was about history and preaching. On Friday, returned to Wrexham. On Saturday, spoke at the funeral of a young woman named Anne Wakefield, aged 24. She was buried at Rhosddu, a very ancient burial-place. On Sunday (30th), preached at the chapel. The church is low, and divided: some of the disciples of Campbell disturb the brethren.

Dec. 31.—Left for home, *via* Shrewsbury and Abergavenny; arrived at 1 p.m.

**1856.**—Preached at home for several Sundays.

Feb. 3.—At Castleton.

Feb. 17.—Preached twice at Cwmera: a happy day.

Feb. 24.—Preached at Llanwenarth twice, also once at Tudor Street: very fair meetings.

March 2.—Preached twice at Crickhowell; cause very low there.

March 10.—Went to hear the eminent Italian, Gavazzi, at the Cymreigyddion Hall. He is a strange-looking man—too theatrical!

March 23.—Preached twice at Bethlehem, Llanelly

March 30.—Preached at Crickhowell: a good day.

April 6.—Communion Sunday. Had a very good meeting in the morning; many present. Preached my farewell sermon in the evening from *Isa.* lxiii. 7. Of that sermon I give the last paragraph: "Here my ministry among you comes to a close. Brethren and hearers, we shall meet again—perhaps not as we are here at present; but we shall meet at the Judgment Day. That will be a solemn meeting. Everyone must give an account of what he did in the flesh: the preacher of his preaching; the professor of his professing; and the hearer for all his hearing. But my conscience testifies within me that I will not be afraid to meet you then. May God give us grace that we may meet in Glory to praise redeeming love when time shall be no more!"

How hard these people! They do not mind that I go away, though they say they are sorry. I have ministered here for eight years and three months. When I began, the church was 39 members—now they are 71; 40 were baptized by me. All the salary I received was £37 a year till I married; after that I had £48 10s. But £8 10s. was paid for the cottage where I lived; so I only had £40 for a family of four and a servant! With all the economy I and my wife could command, I was often in want of money. O Lord, I bless Thee for all Thy goodness while here. Be with me again; forgive me all my sins; give me the Spirit necessary for the work; lead me by Thy counsel; help me to preach the Gospel; and Thine shall be the glory. Amen.

## LLANELLY.

April 13.—Preached twice at Bethlehem. This church gives me a warm invitation to become its pastor—not one member opposed—and I have accepted. My God, I look for help to Thee.

April 20.—Preached twice at Llanelly: very happy day.

April 27.—Preached at Penrose. Paid Mr. Webb £6 I had collected.

April 30.—Mr. William Davies, of the Church Farm, one of the deacons at Llanthewy, removed my furniture to Llanelly without any cost; no damage or accident.

May 4.—Commenced my ministry at the new place; preached twice; Communion. I pray the Lord to smile on me in this place. My salary was promised monthly—about £60 a year. The church is low; there had been divisions in the time of Mr. Dan Davies.

May 5.—Prayer Meeting. 6th, Singing School. 7th, Prayer Meeting. 8th, Preached at the funeral of a poor mother; it was heart-rending to see her little children weeping at the grave. 9th, Prayer Meeting at a private house. Visited many families in order to know the people. 10th, at the funeral of a child.

May 18th.—Preached twice: good. One hopeful woman came on.

May 21 and 22.—At the Annual Meetings of Pontypool College: Rev. J. H. Hinton preached, and the effect of his sermon was truly delightful. He himself once burst into tears and his voice almost failed.

May 27 and 28.—At the Association at Pisgah; some heavy rain: preached the first evening at the "Pilgrim's Rest," Mr. Isaac Hiley's house. There was "hwylus" preaching at this Association.

July 16.—Went to Swansea with my family for better health.

July 20.—Preached twice at Bethesda; again on Wednesday evening, and on the Sunday following. We returned home mid-week, a little better.

Aug. 3.—Preached twice at home; the great heat made us all heavy; for it has been unusually hot for many days.

Aug. 17.—Exchanged with Mr. Williams, Darrenfelen. Wet day.

Aug. 31.—Preached thrice at the S. S. Anniversary at Calvary, Brynmawr; had a good day.

Sept. 1.—With Rev. T. Thomas, the Tutor, at Mrs. Micah Thomas's house. We divided his library between Pontypool and Haverfordwest Colleges: this was the late Micah Thomas's Will.

Sept. 9.—Felt very unwell; consulted the doctor, who said I had fever. 19th, I am able to rise, but am very weak. It is to-day the 24th; have not been out yet, but am recovering. *Laus Deo.*

Sept. 28.—Preached on Sunday evening, though very weak.

Oct. 11.—Married at Bethlehem, George Collett to Rachel Edmunds. Rev. Mr. Edwards, Brynmawr, the Registrar, was present.

Oct. 13.—At Bethlehem, married Wm. Powell to Eliz. Jones, of Brynmawr.

Nov. 15.—Was induced by friends to join the Philanthropic Club.

Dec. 20.—Married at Bethlehem, Wm. Moss to Anne Nicholas.

Christmas Day.—Lectured at Bethlehem on "Siencyn Penhydd." Rev. B. Williams, Darrenfelen, in the chair.

Dec. 28.—The old and well-known minister, Isaac Jones, Staylittle, preached in the evening: it is sad that old ministers must go a-begging!

**1857.** Jan. 11.—Preached twice : Baptism had to be postponed, owing to the water having leaked out of the baptistery.

Jan. 18.—Preached. Baptized two young women. A good day.

Jan. 25.—Preached twice at Crickhowell. Communion.

Feb. 4.—My wife gave birth to a daughter. All well. (This little girl, Mary, died in 1859.)

March 12.—Gave a lecture at the Reading Room on Adam and Eden.

March 29.—Baptized three in the afternoon.

April 11.—Married Howell Thomas to Elizabeth Williams.

April 19.—Preached at "The Royal Oak" P.H., in the afternoon : an old woman there (Mrs. Hiley) is a member. Had no *hwyl.*

April 28.—At Bedwas Quarterly Meeting—two days.

May 26 and 27.—At our Association at Salem, Blaenau : rather a flat affair. Mr. Williams, Darrenfelen, and myself preached the first evening at Berea.

June 10.—At an Eisteddfod at Aberdare : took a 50/- prize for an essay.

[I sent in two other essays, but did not get the prize, but praise instead. One essay was on "Capital Punishment." It is printed in *Seren Gomer*, 1857, pp. 337-346. The other on "The Working Class, etc.," is in *Seren Gomer*, 1858, pp. 346-352, and 392-394.]

June 21.—Baptized one. At the Ordination of Mr. Ingram. At Nazareth in the afternoon. At home at 6.

June 24.—Unbearable heat: yet I have caught a severe cold! Went to Caerphilly and returned next day.

Aug. 10.—Married Thos. Davies to Ann George, both from Brynmawr.

Aug. 12.—At the funeral of an ungodly young man, Joseph Parry (24), who was killed by a limestone wagon running over him.

Aug. 15.—Preached to two Clubs: they gave me 10/-.

Aug. 30.—Went to Parkend, Glos., and preached in a Club Room. Heard Mr. Spurgeon four times the following week (see a full account in *Seren Cymru*, 1857, pp. 368-370).

Sept. 13.—Preached twice at Caersalem, Dowlais; Church very dead.

Sept. 19.—Married two couples from Brynmawr.

Sept. 30.—Went to Crickhowell C. M. Association: heard Revs. Howells, of Swansea, and O. Thomas, of London. My soul was made glad. In the evening attended Thanksgiving meeting at home; never had we better harvest weather than this year. "Let all praise Thee."

Oct. 7 (Wednesday) National Fast and Prayer on behalf of India. We had two meetings.

Oct. 11.—Baptized two in the afternoon: had a happy time.

Oct. 12.—Heard Mr. Guinness at Siloam: very much disappointed.

Oct. 17.—Married Geo. Boles, a Prim. Methodist preacher, to Mary Watkins.

Oct. 27.—Preached at the Brynhyfryd Quarterly Meeting.

Dec. 6.—Preached twice: the low state of trade tells fearfully on our collections. Great reductions have been made in the wages of workmen, and hundreds unemployed.

Dec. 16.—Preached at the Tabernacle, Pontypool; at Pisgah on the Thursday evening; and at Horeb, Blaenavon, Friday evening.

Dec. 20.—Preached twice at Llanwenarth: Tudor Street in afternoon.

Dec. 29.—Preached at Hermon; Blaenau Gwent (30), and Beulah (31). At Abercarn Eisteddfod got £1 for a few stanzas, "Yr Athraw Ffyddlon."

**1858.** Jan. 3.—Preached at Darrenfelen; pretty fair meeting.

Jan. 12.—Went to Brecon to my sister's funeral. She was long afflicted. Buried at Cwmdwr, aged 32 (vide *Seren Cymru*). She left behind a husband and children. [Two others rest there: Ruth, my sister, died Nov. 26th, 1835, aged 8 years. The youngest, Joseph (my only brother), died 30th of same month, aged 3 years. Both died of scarlet fever.]

Jan. 31.—Baptized one, William James, in the afternoon.

Feb. 28.—Preached twice at Pisgah: had much help.

March 6.—Married John Llewellyn to Anne Davis, and Henry Miles to Elizabeth Price.

March 28.—At Parkend: preached morning and evening in English; afternoon in Welsh. There were present a few of the workmen from Llanelly. We had good meetings in a Club Room. No Chapel at Parkend, and the people are "heathen." A remarkable incident occurred here: the Club Room was attached to a large hotel, kept by a man named Inman. He lent the room at the request of two workmen, who had gone there from Llanelly, and who were his customers. After my second visit, I found that Mr. Inman and his wife were under deep impressions. He showed me every kindness, and said, "I will give up this business to save my soul." He did that, and removed towards Coleford, where he was baptized. He wrote a kind letter to me which I have preserved (see my collection, p. 39).

April 10.—At a Philanthropic Conference at Bargoed. Went thence to see Mrs. Edmunds at Caerphilly: preached on Sunday at Tonyfelin, and at Bedwas. Returned home on Monday.

April 25.—Exchanged with Rev. B. Williams, Darrenfelen.

May 23.—Preached at Horeb, Blaenavon: Communion. Baptized two.

May 25 and 26.—At our Association at Nebo, meetings rather flat.

June 5.—William Edwards and Alice Price, both from Brynmawr, were married at our Chapel: each only 17 years of age!

June 9.—Preached at Old Blaenau: very sultry weather.

June 27.—Preached twice; prayer meetings for the revival of the cause here have been held for the past four weeks, and are to be continued. My little girl, Mary Elizabeth is ill, and my son Tom poorly. Trouble comes on all—why not on me?

July 4. I have composed a *Pwnc* on *Daniel* iii., and it has been recited by our S. School, and also Llanwenarth: a success.

July 14.—Preached at the funeral of Margaret Williams, a member, aged 73.

July 18.—Preached in the morning at Llanwenarth. Communion. Old age has conquered Mr. Hiley; he said a few words at the table, and the people were glad to hear his sweet voice. At home in the evening.

July 21.—Preached at the "Blue Boar" P.H. Good meeting, though on unconsecrated ground!

July 25.—Recited our *Pwnc* at Tabor, Brynmawr, at 3 p.m.

July 27 and 28.—At our Quarterly Meeting at Zion, Brynmawr; preached the first evening.

Aug. 29.—Preached at the S.S. Anniversary of Calvary, Brynmawr.

Sept. 5.—Preached thrice: baptized one; am afraid he will not wear well. This proved true—he was John Evans, "Forgehammer" P.H.; he died soon after.

Sept. 13.—My wife was suddenly taken ill, and I have to attend on her day and night. . . . . But I am thankful that her life is spared.

Oct. 6.—Our Thanksgiving meeting for an excellent harvest.

Oct. 7.—The Great Comet appears grandly these last nights; the tail is very long. At first it appeared in the region of Ursa Major, but now it has moved toward the sunset. I pencilled a sketch of it on the fly-leaf of my Hebrew grammar.

Oct. 25.—Thieves broke into our Chapel a few weeks ago and stole all our brass candle-holders. We now appointed persons to collect subscriptions to repair the loss.

Oct. 26.—Went to Llanhiddel Quarterly Meeting. I had there a damp bed, and was very poorly for weeks.

Nov. 23.—Removed from the old house by Llanelly Church to "Vine Cottage." A public house by the Church, with skittle alley, was too much for me to bear; and one night I took away the pins and burnt them; and I had quiet until they got a fresh set. I do not think they ever suspected me.

Dec. 6.—Preached at the funeral of old David Williams, aged 82, buried at our Chapel. His life was far from consistent—the drink! He was baptized at Penyrheol. After all, there was love to Christ in the man, and great humility. I have hope for him.

Christmas Day.—Very wet: had a good meeting in Chapel.

Dec. 31.—Preached in a cottage. I have done much of this since I came here—some meetings almost every night. Preached many times at the Pentre farm-house. Mrs. Morgan is a member, but her husband is a drunkard! I am afraid he will never mend. (He never did.)

1859. Jan. 2.—Preached twice: sermons suitable to the times.

Feb. 13.—Preached at Darrenfelen in the morning, and baptized eight women.

Feb. 27.—Preached thrice: baptized ten persons.

March 6.—Fifteen were added to the Church to-day.

March 13.—Exchanged with Rev. Enoch Price, Crickhowell; returned home the same night: wet. Good service.

March 20.—A good day. A very noted sinner, Lewis Jones, came on : this man was in a good position in the works: he was shrewd and talented, but he was a professed infidel, who had never been to a place of worship for 17 years. He told me he cursed Chapel-goers in his very heart; he was immoral and unkind to his family. He received a letter from his sister in America, and something in that brought him to our Chapel. He was converted, and when he came on one Sunday night he wept and trembled. He said, "I have served the devil most faithfully, and I hope now to serve Christ." He was a master blacksmith, and made an iron railing for our baptistery in which he was baptized. He behaved well as far as I knew him : he spoke well, and used to preach at times. In two or three years he went to America, and I heard no more about him. He was a monument of grace, and all wondered at the change in him.

March 27.—Baptized eleven persons: may they prove true.

March 30. — Have finished my translation of Spurgeon's Sermons. I have been at this work eighteen months; have written 592 pages. Eleven numbers contain sermons, and the twelfth contains a history of Mr. Spurgeon to the present time. The book has sold well, although I had only £4 or £5 out of it.

April 3.—Preached thrice at Brynhyfryd; exchanged with Mr. Johns.

April 17.—Did not go out all day; watched my dear little girl dying—a most affectionate and knowing child. She suffered much from convulsions for three days before her death, at the age of two years and three months.

April 18 (Monday).—She expired this morning at 1.10 p.m. Happy child, now with Christ; but thy parents weeping!

April 20.—My dear little girl is in her coffin; she looks well; there is a smile and calmness now on her face; she seems to gaze with delight on some wondrous scene of glory and bliss unseen by me. Oh, this little body! it holds connection with Heaven; the Spirit is there. Oh, my dear child, I nursed thee tenderly and dearly; not a day passed without thee! How fond she was of me! When in my study, she would call me at the foot of the stairs. Every day she came up to me and amused herself with books and pictures. She was the first downstairs with me every morning. I always dressed her, and washed her hands and face. But now—she is for ever made clean and white in the Lamb's Blood. I bid her adieu on Sunday; she noticed me then, and although she did not understand me, yet I told her we only part for a while: "I shall see thee again, and never after part." O my Father, Thou gavest her to me: I did for her what I could. She was taken from us to praise the great Redeemer, and she had to see Him before she ever learnt of Him. Oh, happy child! Lord, be with me and mine; help, oh, help us! Precious is the religion of Christ. What could I do without the light of Thy Word shed over the regions of death? I now behold the glorious morn of the resurrection, when I shall meet my dear Mary without her sufferings. Ah, cruel death! then I shall trample thee under my feet, even as thou didst trample under thy iron foot my dear child. Hallelujah! the Jubilee is hastening! Between 5 and 6 o'clock our dear Mary was buried at Bethlehem, in blessed hope waiting the advent of Jesus Christ.

----

### LITTLE MARY IN HEAVEN.

I saw her live—a sweet, engaging child,
Her beauty great, her smile serene and mild.
I saw her die—alas! how hard the day
When, dearest child, thou hadst to pass away!
I see her now—she stands before the Throne,
A happy guest in God's eternal home.
She's glad—for every sorrow now is past;
To the eternal rest she's come at last.
She smiles—for holy angels stand around;
Their joy and bliss for ever there abound.
She shouts for joy—the Saviour is her Friend;
Her pain is o'er—her songs shall never end.

----

April 24.—Though weak, I preached twice, and baptized seven persons.

May 22.—Preached in the morning at Llanwenarth. Mr. Johns baptized sixteen persons. I had help in a wonderful degree during the past weeks. I had to prepare for the examination of the Pontypool students in Classics, and write a letter in English and Welsh for the Association; subject, " The New Testament Christian."

G

May 24 and 25.—The Association was held at Bethlehem, in fine weather; great power attended most of the sermons. This was emphatically one of the best Associations remembered by any living—to God be the glory!

June 27.—Preached at the re-opening of Hermon, Nantyglo.

July 3.—Preached thrice at Jerusalem, Rhymney.

July 10.—Preached twice at home; hot weather, and meetings heavy.

July 16.—Phillip Davies, son of Rev. Jas. Davies, Brynmawr, was married to Ruth Eynon at our chapel. Rev. Jas. Davies and his family are going to America.

July 20.—Heard Mr. Spurgeon preach at Castleton.

Aug. 14.—Preached twice, and baptized five persons. We recited our *Pwnc* at Crickhowell in the afternoon.

Aug. 28.—Preached thrice at Calvary, Brynmawr.

Sept. 4.—Preached twice. We recited our *Pwnc* at Llanwenarth.

Sept. 25.—The anniversary of our Sabbath school; Rev. E. Price preached. I went to Crickhowell by 6 p.m.; walked home alone in a dark night; home by ten.

Oct. 9.—Preached at Jerusalem, Rhymney; had much freedom.

Nov. 6.—Again at Jerusalem; very stormy and wet all day; Communion in the evening. I have settled to go there. "O Lord, remember me."

Nov. 14.—My old friend, Mr. David Lewis, son of Rev. Jas. Lewis, Llanwenarth, died. [See his memoir in the *Bedyddiwr*, 1866.]

Nov. 24.—My wife gave birth to a daughter at 10 p.m. The Lord is a present help in time of need.

Dec. 4.—Preached at Jerusalem twice, and baptized one person.

Dec. 25 (Christmas Day).—My last Sunday here; had much help and kindness from all. I resign in the spirit of the Gospel: I leave because the works are likely to stop for ever. I have been very comfortable here, and the church has become strong. The chapel needed enlarging; but the commercial outlook is bad: nearly all must go away, or remain and be very poor.

Dec. 29.—I finished my second reading of the Hebrew Psalms. During my ministry at Bethlehem I wrote 7 volumes of Sermons, containing 340 discourses and 1,214 pages; besides which, I have 7 volumes of English and Welsh mixed; 21 volumes were written at Llanthewy. I hope to go over them all again.

During my time here and at Llanthewy I wrote very many papers for our magazines and *Seren Cymru.*

During some of the time at Llanelly I had a weekly class in chapel of young men who studied English grammar, and the rudiments of general knowledge. In another class we went through Mr. Richd. Mills' grammar of music.

I also had a " Singing School " to improve our Sunday worship. After two years, one Wm. Williams relieved me as far as the music went. One of the young men, a member, named Joshua James, presented me with "Neander's Church History"; and the Sunday school gave me £5.

RHYMNEY (MON.)..

**1860.** Jan. 1.—Preached twice at Jerusalem. Good attendance, though very wet. Communion in evening. Began my ministry here—may the Lord be pleased to bless us. Salary promised £6 per month—13 in the year.

This week I spent at Llanelly : attended meetings, and preached once : visited the people, and had some hours at Hebrew.

Jan. 7.—Walked to Rhymney: at a Temperance meeting in the evening.

Jan. 8.—Preached twice at Jerusalem : and at Zoar at 4. On Monday at 3, Prayer Meetings — Union Prayer Meetings held in rotation at the Chapels, and there is some move among the people.

Jan. 15.—Preached at Bethlehem, Llanelly, thrice ; baptized three persons. There are now sixteen before the Church.

Jan. 16.—At the Society at Bethlehem in the evening ; there are now twenty before the Church. I praise the Lord for what He has done for Bethlehem.

Jan. 17.—We removed our goods and chattels to Rhymney. Attended a large meeting in the evening.

Jan. 29.—Preached thrice ; baptized nine, and restored nine.

Feb. 5.—Preached twice at Bethlehem ; baptized twenty-four—among whom were a Wesleyan and an Independent : a good day.

Feb. 9.—Wrote an article " Asgell " for Mathetes' *Geiriadur*. Was at our singing school in the evening.

Feb. 26.—Preached twice, and baptized nineteen persons.

March 4.—Preached at Tirphil : we here start a new cause.

March 5.—At the re-opening of Penuel, Twyncarno ; collected £120 10s.

March 24.—Translated Dies Irae, which shall appear in *Seren Cymru* (see also the *Greal*, 1867, pp. 224-227).

March 25.—Baptized twenty-one, and restored eight. [From this point I shall notice no more baptisms till the end.]

May 22 and 23.—At the Annual Meetings of Pontypool College, which passed fairly well.

May 29 and 30.—At Abercarn Association : this was Mr. Spurgeon's Association—20,000 people present, a grand sight ! I wrote a leader to *Seren Cymru* on the Association.

June 11.—A Church was formed at Tirphil to-day.

June 19 and 20.—At Mill St., Aberdare, Association. I had been asked to preach ; which I did in Welsh and English (Text 1 *Peter* i. 11). I am thankful that the Lord greatly helped me.

July 3.—Preached in English in a wooden shed at Maes-y-cwmmer : the starting of an English cause here. I stayed with Mr. Llew. Jenkins.

July 14.—Wrote " Adonai " for Mathetes' *Geiriadur*.

July 17.—Wrote another article on " Adwaen."

July 20.—At Penuel in the morning. Communion. Mr. Jones being in London. Walked to Caersalem, Dowlais, and preached at 6. Mr. Evans came down from the Wells that night.

Aug. 19.—At Charles Street, Newport, the cause is low, indeed!

Aug. 26.—Preached at Zion, Merthyr : had much help. A wet and bad harvest this year ; and no wonder—sin abounds!

Sept. 2.—At Anniversary at Felinfoel, Carmarthenshire : Brethren John, of Llangyndeirne, and Jenkins, of Trefdraeth, preached with me. At Soho on Monday, and preached at the Chapel at 7 p.m.

Sept. 30.—Preached thrice at Tirphil. I was the first to preach in the new Chapel : good meetings and large congregations.

Oct. 19.—At the funeral of the eminent Francis Hiley, of Llanwenarth ; many ministers were present. He died in his 80th year.

Oct. 28 and 29.—Preached at the Anniversary of Mill Street, Aberdare : Revs. Hughes, Dinas ; Jones, Carmarthen ; and Roberts, Merthyr ; were the other preachers. Good services.

Oct. 30.—Heard Rev. Mr. Stephens, Dwygyfylden, lecture on Music at Zion, Rhymney. Excellent : his singing very impressive.

Nov. 30.—Finished my exposition and translation of the *Book of Joel* after four months' hard work. Gave it in lectures to my people. [It is printed in the

Quarterly *Seren Gomer*, 1861, pp. 15-31, 102-120, 199-207, and 1862, pp. 18-41.]

Dec. 27.—Wrote "Ymddiddan rhwng offeiriad a gweithiwr" for *Seren Cymru*. Very racy papers—no doubt some will kick, but I am unknown.

I did much at Hebrew through this year. A young man named Shedaski, a Prussian Jew who was a good Hebraist, called with me often. He professed Christianity, and I taught him English in exchange for his Hebrew.

Through the year I attended a very large number of meetings of all kinds. I had classes in Chapel to instruct young men in Reading, Writing Welsh, Grammar and Biblical Geography. One studied Greek and Hebrew. Read proof sheets of Mathetes' *Geiriadur* at his request. (I did this for some years; he expected me to look after the Hebrew and Greek.) Much sickness this year in my family: mother and children often down; and I paid more doctors' bills than ever before.

Vol. I. of my sermons was written: they number 94, and fill 472 pages.

1861. Jan. 1.—"Be Thou with me this year, O Jehovah!"

Jan. 6.—While I was preaching, Mr. David John, a member, was called out of Chapel and taken in charge of a policeman, on an accusation of defrauding a club. It was a cold, frosty night, and the constable had exceeded his duty. It was a case of revenge, and our brother got free. Mr. John was a most inoffensive man, and his arrest created a sensation.

Feb. 10.—Preached thrice at Beulah, and baptized nine.

Feb. 28.—This was to me one of the hardest days of my life: I visited 38 families, and visiting at best is not my delight, though it pleases some people.

Mar. 9.—Writing an article on " Anadl " for the *Geiriadur.*

Mar. 18.—A Committee was formed in the place to effect, if possible, the closing of public houses on Sundays.

Mar. 31.—At Hengoed—having exchanged with Mr. Williams.

April 1.—Heard Rev. T. Price, Aberdare, lecture for three hours at Zoar on " Garibaldi."

May 8.—Cold rain and heavy snow! 13th, Re-opening of Bargoed Chapel.

May 21 and 22.—At the Annual Meetings of Pontypool College: they were well attended. Fine weather.

May 26.—Preached at home at Penuel ; baptized 4.

May 27.—Preparing a short lecture on the history of the Arabs.

May 28 and 29.—At our Association at Blaenavon ; preached in English at 7 p.m. ; fine weather.

June 1.—Delivered my lecture on the Arabs, at our Chapel. I was assisted by Youhanah El Karey (an Arab convert), who did what he could with his scanty English (Mr. Karey is now head of the Baptist Mission Station at Nablous).

June 6.—Finished the reading of Dr. Wayland's " Principles of the Baptists." A most excellent book : it abounds in valuable suggestions.

June 10.—Wrote " Anfonedig "—a short article for the *Geiriadur*.

June 27.—Heard Mr. Spurgeon preach twice at Cardiff. Tremendous thunderstorm at 3 : yet good meetings.

July 5.—Translated one of Mr. Spurgeon's sermons for Rev. Moses Roberts, of Felinfoel : to help his book to go. This I did as a labour of love.

July 15 and 16.—At Horeb, Blaenavon : Rev. James Richards, of Pontypridd, preached a most wonderful sermon for 1½ hours from *Rev.* i. 4, etc. Mr. Johns, of Llanwenarth, and myself tried to preach, but we felt small.

July 19.—Went to Carmarthen, and preached at the Tabernacle.

July 20.—Went to Cardigan. 21st, Preached twice at Bethania ; Communion service in the morning.

July 22.—Went to St. Dogmells to see Rev. J. P. Williams, formerly of Pantycelyn—his mind is gone— the end is near.

July 24.—Youhanah El Karey was here ; I helped him at his meetings at Bethania and Penypark. Crowds followed him : he was quite a show in his Eastern costume.

July 28.—Preached twice at Bethania : at Penypark at 2.

Aug. 10.—Finished reading the Pentateuch in Hebrew.

Aug. 18.—Preached twice at Llanwenarth, and in town in afternoon.

Aug. 19.—At Llanelly : visited about 32 houses : Society at Bethlehem.

Sep. 1.—Preached on the error of " Sprinkling." 3rd, Prepared article on " Sprinkling " for the *Bedyddiwr.*

Nov. 26.—Have now read my Hebrew Bible to *Judges.*

Nov. 27.—About 200 of us from the Chapel followed the funeral of Miss Davies, grocer, who was buried at Hengoed.

Dec. 2.—At the opening of the Temperance Hall at Tredegar.

Dec. 6 and 7.—Heard Rev. Mr. Hughes, of Penmain, deliver two lectures on " Sprinkling," at Moriah Chapel. I asked permission to reply to him in the same place : but got no reply.

Dec. 21.—Delivered my reply to Mr. Hughes at our Chapel—very well received by the large assembly.

Dec. 22.—Preached at Siloh, Tredegar ; also gave an address on Temperance at the Temperance Hall at 5 p.m.

Dec. 23.—Gave my reply to Mr. Hughes, Penmain, at Siloh. I did much at Hebrew this year, and made some progress in German : went through the Course in Cassell's " Popular Educator," and wrote a German Grammar for myself ! Read " Herodotus," and found it very interesting—I had one volume of it in Greek. Religion was more dead in this year than the last, yet we have less cause to complain than many. We have had much stir about Baptism. (I published two tracts which appear in the *Bedyddiwr* for 1861, pp. 293 and 357.) May the Truth be the Ruler among Christians. The great events of this year were the war in America for the liberation of the slaves, and the death of Prince Albert the Good.

Vol. 2 contains my sermons of the year: they number 77, covering 320 pp. I pray God to bless what was preached, that the seed may have deep soil, and much fruit in time to come. Amen.

1862. Jan. 12.—An English Baptist Church has been formed here to-day. I preached for them at two p.m. They meet in an old empty grocer's shop.

Jan. 22.—Rev. John Evans, of Abercanaid, was here with me all day. He preaches in the place, and sells his sermons. A good old brother he, though odd in manner.

Jan. 26.—Preached twice. When in the pulpit in the evening a terrible temptation rushed upon me. The Church owed me £4, and the Devil put it into my mind that the Church did not care about me. I was tempted to leave the pulpit then and walk out. While singing before the sermon the lines—

> " Gair fy Nuw sy'n drech nâ'r moroedd,
>  Gair fy Nuw sy'n drech nâ'r don," etc.,

I had help, and my mind had rest. All passed well to the end.

Feb. 24.—When in the chair at Siloh, Tredegar—Youhanah El Karey having begun his Arab lecture—I was called out and ordered home at once. When I arrived I found an addition of a daughter to the household—and all well. (She is Margaret Anne (Maggie), and became the wife of a Missionary under the American Bap. Mission in India.)

Feb. 26.—Attended the great meeting at High Street Chapel, Merthyr Tydfil, in connection with the bi-centenary of the 2,000 ejected ministers.

March 20.—Finished my article on "Baal" for Mathetes' *Geiriadur*.

March 29.—Wrote Miles Edwards' Memoir for *Seren Cymru*. ("Rufus" republished it in his History of the Colleges, p. 17.)

April 2.—My dear brother, Daniel Morgan, Blaen-avon, and I went to a committee at Aberdare.

April 5.—Wrote for the *Seren Cymru*.

April 6.—Preached at Siloh, Tredegar, and collected for the Bible Translation Society. Heard Lord Teynham preach at three p.m.—a plain, good old man.

April 17.—Went to Liverpool Association. Preached at Gt. Cross Hall Street. (18th) Preached at ten at Athol; at two at Stanhope; six at Gt. Cross Hall Street. (22nd) Public meeting at Byrom; many spoke, I in English. (24th) Preached at Gt. Cross Hall Street. (25th) Preached at Stanhope. (27th, Sunday) Preached at Gt. Cross Hall Street, morning and evening; at Crown Street at two p.m. Began my way home on Monday, and arrived in the evening. I feel very thankful to the Lord for His goodness and for the help vouchsafed.

May 7.—Have helped Abel Edmunds to put in order the History of the Baptists at Rhymney. (He published the whole in a little book, for which I re-wrote all the matter.)

May 20 and 21.—At the Annual Meetings of Ponty-pool College. Mr. Lloyd, of Merthyr, was the Welsh preacher; very good.

May 27 and 28.—At the Association at Bassalleg—one of the poorest I ever attended.

June 7 (Saturday).—On foot to Merthyr, thence by train to Neath. Walked with the Rev. Wm. Harris, Aberdare, to Llwyni, nearly 10 miles, over an un-known and rough road, by Pontrhydyfen and Penhydd —the home of Shencin. Arrived at our journey's end at seven p.m.

June 8 (Sunday).—Preached at ten with Rev. James Richards, who had the evening service to himself. He preached with wonderful power. On Monday at ten Mr. Richards again alone; Mr. Harris and myself at two and six. Very excellent meetings. It was Mr. Richards' desire to be alone; and indeed he was right. I never heard his equal.

June 10.—Turned my steps once again home-wards, walked to Neath, and arrived safely at sundown.

June 12.—Wrote an article for *Seren Cymru.*

June 22.—Preached to my old friends at Bethlehem. Communion.

July 21. Began to prepare my reply to Hughes, Penmain, for the Press. (I finished it Aug. 7th. Published at 6d., and sold well.)

Aug. 14.—At the opening of the New Baptist Chapel at Llanwrtyd Wells; slept one night with my old friends the Winstons.

Aug. 17.—Preached at Pantycelyn at 10, at Salim at 2, at the Bont at 6, where I preached in English and Welsh.

Aug. 19.—Preached at Horeb, Cwmdwr; slept at Cwmyronen, my father's old house.

Aug. 20.—Preached at the Baptist Chapel, Llandovery: while here I found the lease of Horeb, which had been lost for 30 years: thus the Chapel was saved from the landlord who was intending to take it for the Church of England.

Aug. 24.—Preached from a text appropriate to the 2000 ejected, and the service passed well.

Sept. 8 (and following days).—Spoke at several Bicentenary Meetings; distributed my reply to Hughes by post and hand.

Sept. 29.—Wrote " Pregeth i 'ffeirad " for the *Seren Cymru.*

Oct. 24.—Brother Robt. Ellis preached his parting sermon at our Chapel: he is leaving for Carnarvon. I am sorry to lose the company of so good a man.

Nov. 11.—At the ordination of Mr. John Morgan, at Pontygwaith, Tredegar.

Nov. 16.—Preached twice: had much help. O that the people were up to my spirit, poor as I am!

Dec. 28 (Sunday).—Communion in the evening. I was to have baptized several in the afternoon, but the deacons neglected the baptistery at the rock: there was no water in it; it would take long to fill: there was a crowd present—largely Irish, to whom I was compelled to explain that the ordinance would be postponed to another day. For once I lost all self-control, and felt indignant and enraged at the careless-ness of my people. What a spree our enemies had! How I saw them laugh and mock! I thought of my zeal for the ordinance, and of the indifference of the deacons, and that made me wild. I had told them in the morning to mind the water, so they had no excuse. When I returned home I was half dead: and had it not been our Communion I would not have gone to Chapel at 6. However, I preached, tho' excitedly. At the close of the service I referred to the neglect. Each culprit put the blame on the other; but I told the Church that my Pastorate ended that night: but I would preach for them for a few Sundays—and no more.

They did all they could to smooth over the blunder, but I would not give way. In less than a fortnight I had several requests to supply pulpits with a view to the Pastorate.

Vol. III. contains my written sermons for this year; they number 73, and contain 320 pp. I was from home ten Sundays throughout the year; I preached 149 times. The Churches were all rather dead, but I had much pleasure in preaching often. "Yn drag'wyddol y'th folianaf."

1863. Jan. 1.—"Here I begin another year. What changes I may see I know not; but I pray that I may be led by Thee, O my God!

Jan. 5.—At the funeral of an old minister, Rev. Daniel Jones, Tongwynlas, aged 75. A large number present.

Jan. 7.—Very much hindered by frequent callers during the day.

Jan. 13.—At the funeral of dear Mrs. Edmunds, Caerphilly, aged 86. She was buried with her family at Llysfaen. (See her memoir in *Seren Gomer*, 1864, pp. 23-28. It contains a letter from Rev. Jas. Richards.)

Jan. 29.—At Caerphilly. Sold most of the effects in Mrs. Edmunds' house. House, contents, and some other property had been willed to my wife.

March 1.—Preached at Priory St. Chapel, Carmarthen.

March 3.—Preached at Ffynon, and visited Trefangor.

March 4.—Preached at Rhydwilym. 5th, Preached for the Welsh at Haverfordwest. 6th, Preached at Bethlehem, a short distance out. 8th, Preached thrice at Hill Park; had good meetings. This Church gives me a call. 9th, Preached at Carmarthen : there is a call here. I thank the Lord for helping me. 10th, Reached home by 7.30 p.m.

March 17.—Wrote a short memoir of my dear young friend, Mr. Joshua James, of Llanelly, for *Seren Cymru*. He gave me 10 vols. of " Neander's Church History."

March 28.—Went to Carmarthen : had a melancholy sight. I gazed upon the charred and blackened house of Mr. David Lewis, merchant, which had been totally destroyed by fire the previous night. The family had a narrow escape. Mr. Lewis and his wife are members at Priory Street.

March 29.—Preached at Peniel; have accepted the invitation of this Church. I took a house *pro tem.* in Union Street, as I could not get one nearer the Chapel.

April 5.—Preached twice at Jerusalem : both people and myself felt sorry to part.

April 19.—Preached twice at Jerusalem. Communion. Finished my ministry here—felt it very deeply. During my time here I baptized 84 persons : a few, I fear disappointed us. My previous baptisms were 40 at Llanthewy, and 61 at Llanelly. Vol. 4 to p. 96 contains my sermons at Jerusalem, 19 in number.

April 26.—Visited the old friends at Cwmera : preached twice ; at Gelly in the morning.

April 27.—Went to Llanthewy and Abergavenny to bid farewell to old faces.

April 28.—At Salem, Blaenau Quarterly Meeting : preached in the evening. (See my dismission letter.)

## CARMARTHEN.

1863. May 1.—Removed our effects from Rhymney to Carmarthen. I and my little family reached the town in the evening, and stayed with Mrs. Bowen at the "White Horse."

May 3.—Commenced my ministry ; preached twice. Communion. Good meetings. (Here I preach twice on Sunday, and once during every week.)

May 19 and 20.—At the Quarterly Meeting at Salem, Meidrym. A bad start. In the Conference I had to oppose Revs. B. Williams and H. W. Jones : they found fault with the committee for allowing Mr. Llew. Jenkins £10 per cent. for collecting for the Welsh Building Fund. I was the only member of that committee present. They yielded.

H

June 9 and 10.—At the Association at New Quay. I preached in English and Welsh.

June 21.—Preached at Ffynonhenry, and baptized three persons: at Rhydargaeau at 2 and 6.

Aug. 22.—At the Tabernacle I married Geo. Bowen to Mary Jenkins. I deputised for Rev. H. W. Jones, who was away.

Aug. 30.—Being at Llanwrtyd Wells as a companion to my dear friend David Lewis, merchant, I rode over to Pantycelyn. On the journey the horse stumbled; I fell, and hurt my right shoulder very much. I was not able to proceed, but turned to Brynarth, a farm hard by, where I was known. I preached at Salim in the afternoon, and at Llanwrtyd at 6. I had my arm the while in a sling. It was very painful the next day, and I returned to Carmarthen.

Sept. 6.—Preached twice at home, my arm still in a sling.

Sept. 28.—Removed from Union Street to No. 14, Quay Street.

Oct. 25 and 26.—Preached at Narberth Anniversary. Dr. Davies, of Haverfordwest, and Mr. Short, of Swansea, preached with me; they in English, and I in Welsh.

Nov. 16.—Began my "Esboniad y Teulu": wrote a short preface to *Genesis*. I was engaged on this work for seven years.

Nov. 26.—At *Genesis*, but a bad headache drove study away.

Dec. 11.—Wrote an article, "Cabbalistiaid" for the *Geiriadur*.

Dec. 19.—Jackey Howell, aged 81, an old member, was buried at St. David's. He used to ride on a little donkey to the Chapel door, then his daughter carried him in and put him in his seat. His heart was weak, but he would come to Chapel. What an example!

**1864.**—The past year has been noted for deadness in the Churches. I baptized a few, and we had plenty of meetings, some very profitable.

Jan. 24.—Walked to Rhydargaeau. Communion. Caught cold and was laid up with bronchitis for weeks.

Feb. 17.—Our Quarterly Meeting—it ended opportunely; for " Unto us a child is born, unto us a son is given." All well.

March 26.—Went to Swansea, and preached at Bethlehem.

Anniversary Meeting; Rev. R. A. Jones preached with me. On Sunday, preached at Trinity Calv. Meth. Chapel at 3. Dr. Thomas Rees preached with me; and Ienan Gwyllt introduced the service. Morning and evening at Bethlehem. On Monday at 7 p.m., Mr. Roberts, Llwynhendy, and I preached at Dr. Rees's Chapel.

June 14 and 15.—At Rhydargaeau Association: Williams of Aberystwyth excelled.

June 21 and 22.—At the Swansea Association: Dr. Price and I preached in English at Mount Pleasant.

Aug. 15.—Spent most of this week at Llangollen College: examined the Students in Greek and Hebrew. Preached in English to the students: Robert Jones in Welsh.

Aug. 29.—Visited a Convict at the County Gaol. I did the same thing many times while at Carmarthen.

Oct. 7.—At the funeral of good old Mr. Morris, M.P., at the Cemetery.

Nov. 21.—Prepared an article on " Cerddoriaeth " for the *Geiriadur.*

Nov. 29.—Visited the Venerable Dd. Evans, Ffynon-henry.

Dec. 6.—Sent an article on Rev. Stephen Davies to Mr. Jos. T. Jones for his *Geiriadur Bywgraffiol.* During this year I attended a large number of meetings in this and other towns (for particulars see my diaries).

**1865.** Jan. 1.—Preached twice. " Gracious Father ! be with me this year, and bless me in my work." O for a revival !

Jan. 25.—Commenced reading the Zurich letters, 4 vols., which are both interesting and profitable.

Feb. 20.—Wrote an article on " Cigfrain " for the *Geiriadur.*

March 8.—Visited Llanddowror, the small, old Church being about to be rebuilt : the old edifice is tumbling down. I stood in the old pulpit of the eminent Griffith Jones, who died in 1761, aged 78. He is buried within the Church. Madame Bevan is there also. They did infinite good by teaching the Welsh to read the Bible.

April 26.—Heard with horror of the assassination of the good President Lincoln. May the Lord have mercy on America.

May 18.—Preached twice at Ffynonhenry, and once at Rhydargaeau : somewhat tiring work.

May 28.—We began preaching in the open air in the back streets of the town: we had a portable pulpit. Profr. Morgan, of Union Street, preached with me to-day.

May 30.—Preached to the students of Haverfordwest College. Mathetes in Welsh.

June 14 and 15.—At the Association at Penrhiwcoch. Good meetings, fine weather. Preached in English at 10.

July 4 and 5.—At Rhydwilym Quarterly Meeting: preached in Welsh at 10.

July 13.—Removed from No. 14 to 25, Quay Street. 28th, Finished the Pentateuch. 30th, Preached at the Independent Chapel, Pentretygwyn; and at a farm named Troedyrhiw in the evening. My Uncle Davies, an old man, dwells there, and I preached in my native air.

Oct. 20.—Heard the able Thomas Binney, of London, at Llanelly: he is an uncommon man.

Nov. 6.—Heard Dr. Wm. Rees (Hiraethog) at Lammas Street Chapel.

Dec. 5.—Mrs. Micah Thomas, of Abergavenny, died at 2 p.m.; her age was 79 years.

Dec. 31.—Preached twice at home, and at Rhydargaeau at 2 p.m. Vol. 4, pp. 97-420, contains all the sermons written from my settlement here to the end of 1865. As I was at the Esboniad every week, I gathered a large store of matter for sermons. I found the expository discourses the best, and the people enjoyed them.

1866.—Still the same prayer:—" May the Lord help and bless me throughout this year."

Jan. 11.—Dry cold weather. The *London* was wrecked in the Bay of Biscay, when about 220 persons perished!

March 9.—At the funeral of Rev. David Evans: he was buried at Ffynonhenry, where he had ministered for about 55 years. Age 88: he was unique. I spoke at his grave. Myfyr Emlyn wrote his memoir.

April 13.—Attended a public meeting of the National Eisteddfod, and spoke.

June 12 and 13.—Preached in English at our Association at Llandilo.

June 19.—A runaway couple—James Christopher (22), farmer, Longland, near Newport, Mon., and Elizabeth Roberts (21), were married by license at our Chapel.

July 14.—Buried Anne James (Nanno Fach), aged 91, at the Chapel: she was a very godly old member, and religion was her chief joy.

Aug. 10.—At a meeting of the Endowed Schools.

Sept. 14.—At another meeting of the same. 24th, Wrote a letter to the *Welshman* (see copy, pp. 5 and 6).

Oct. 11.—Preached in the Chapel, and baptized ten, among whom was my son Tom.

Dec. 29.—The year closes, and I find myself dabbling in too many things, and that my preaching is losing ground. This will never do! I must reform. I have attended this year many Committees of the National Eisteddfod, to be held in this town next year. Also many Committees *re* the Lancasterian Schools, and the Endowed School. Many in the town died of cholera this year—some of our members. (See Diary.)

**1867.**—"O Lord, abide with me!"

Feb. 1.—Translating "Gray's Bard": difficult, but grand.

Feb. 15.—Reading *Hanes Cymru*, by Carnhuanawc.

March 11.—Went to Merthyr Tydfil, with Rev. Latimer Jones, Vicar of S. Peter, on behalf of the National Eisteddfod. It was a foolish step—did no good, but the Vicar would go.

April 16.—Wrote a letter to the *Welshman.* 24th, Eisteddfod Committee ; Mr. Brinley Richards was present.

June 3.—Percy was born, suddenly ; all well.

June 11 and 12.—At our Association at Glanymor, Llanelly. Preached.

June 14.—A Conference at the Assembly Rooms. Miall, Morley, and Hy. Richard there.

June 30.—Preached twice at the Town Hall, our Chapel being closed for cleaning and repainting. What a change! Our forefathers were dragged to such a place to be fined or condemned. Thank God for such peaceable times.

Aug. 25.—Ended our sojourn at the Town Hall.

Aug. 27 and 28.—The first meeting of the Welsh Baptist Union was held here. A large attendance and good effect. I alone was responsible for its coming here, and I was much afraid of the expense ; but the friends unitedly rallied round, and we had no trouble. These meetings were held at the Tabernacle, as it was not deemed prudent to crowd the newly-painted Peniel before the work had fairly set.

Sep. 1.—Preached twice; the first service since the closing in June.

Sep. 2.—The whole of this week was taken by the Nat. Eisteddfod. The weather was very wet and stormy throughout, yet thousands attended. There was a deficit. Carmarthen will not see the Eisteddfod again for a long time. I lost much time during the past 12 months on this account.

Dec. 13 to 22.—Being very unwell I did next to nothing. Weather very severe. This year I had much to do with opening the way to establish an English Baptist Church in the town (see Letter Cuttings in Collection). I also held a large number of Temperance Meetings here and elsewhere. It has been all round a busy year. During the early part of it (in April) it was suggested that my salary be increased from £80 to £96 a year. The senior deacon opposed it. My friend, Mr. David Lewis, merchant, strongly supported the motion for increase, and said that it could easily be done, but the senior deacon was obdurate. The truth is that he was against me, as I had always opposed his overbearing conduct, and we had been obliged to expel his brother—a well-to-do merchant—for getting drunk. Although the Church meeting decided on the increase, our obstinate brother would still not yield, but demanded that the matter be brought before the whole Church at the next Communion! This was granted him, and (April 28) after the Ordinance in the morning I placed the whole matter before the Church. Brother D. Lewis read the resolution passed at the Church meeting. All in favour of the resolution were requested to remain seated, and those against to stand. Our misguided brother jumped up in a rage and said, "Stand all on your feet," to which about 15 members (mostly his relatives) responded. This silenced him, and showed that the Church was with me. I had thought better things of our brother. I hope he will keep his place henceforth, and that this—to him—bitter experience will result in a blessing.

**1868.** How solemn the beginning of another year! What trials and changes may be before me! "Help me to trust in Thee, O Lord, and be faithful in Thy work!"

Jan. 26.—Preached at Llangyndeyrn and Meinciau, though feeling far from well. On the Monday returned through Llandyfeilog, and visited the grave of Peter Williams, author of the great family Bible in Wales. The following is from his tomb :—

"Underneath are deposited the remains of the Rev. Peter Williams, late of Gellilednes, in this parish. All his labors were invariably devoted to promote the temporal and eternal welfare of his countrymen, for whose benefit he published three editions of the Welsh Bible, with explanatory notes, and one edition in 8vo, also a concordance and a number of pamphlets in the same language ; in return for which, alas ! he experienced nothing but persecution and ingratitude ! He continued a faithful and laborious minister of the Gospel for 53 years, and died rejoicing in his God, Aug. 9, 1796, aged 76 years. 'Canys nid gelyn a'm difenwodd,' etc. (*Psa.* lv. 12).

"Mary, his wife, died March 8, 1822, aged 98 years."

Feb. 6.—Wrote a short paper on "Dr. Thomas, Pontypool," for the *Gwyliedydd*, at the request of Rev. B. Evans, Neath.

March 13.—First prayer meeting of the English Baptists held in the Tabernacle Vestry. These meetings continued until a Church was formed. I was with them weekly, and gave a short English address. My chief supporter at first was Mr. Roberts, the ironmonger, and his family.

April 15.—Wrote a letter to the *Welshman*. (See Collection, p. 81.)

May 4.—My wife and children returned after having spent three weeks at Llandilo recruiting their health.

June 9 and 10.—At Verwig Association. Preached at Ffynonbedr and at the Association. Preached at Peniel on the Thursday.

Aug. 18 to 20.—At the Baptist Union at Pwllheli. Preached at several places before my return home. (See Diary.) Home on 31st.

Nov. 1.—Preached at ten. A little girl was born in our family.

Nov. 17.—Thanks that the election is over ; it took much of my time for weeks. Colonel Stepney, our Liberal, got in with 1,297 votes above Tory Treherne. The grandest victory was, however, in the county. Sartoris at the head of the poll on Nov. 24. Now I and my friends breathe freely.

Nov. 20.—Preached at the Union to the poor at 2.30. The ministers of the town go there in turn, and do this without pay. The clergy do not approve of it, although Rev. Latimer Jones has fallen in with us. Not so the old Archdeacon.

Vol. V. contains my sermons to the end of this year. They are 167 in number, and cover 443 pp. The most part of the expository discourses are not included, as they are only outlines for the time.

**1869.**—I pray still for the Divine blessing on my ministry.

Jan. 5.—Signed the Deed of the English Baptists at the office of Mr. J. H. Barker.

Feb. 25.—The continuous mental labour is telling on me. I have frequent severe headaches, which prevent all study.

May 28.—At the funeral of poor Owens, Ffynonhenry, aged 41.

June 8 and 9.—At Llandovery Association. Good "Cymanfa."

July 3.—Wrote a letter to the *Weekly Reporter* "for the benefit of Rev. Latimer Jones." (See Copy in Collection.)

July 5.—Delivered my lecture at our Chapel on "Luther and the Reformation"—with musical illustrations by the choir—which resulted in getting £14 for our Sunday School.

Aug. 24 to 26.—At the Baptist Union at Llanelly. Hot weather.

Sept. 24, etc.—Spent several days in revising Harris's Hymn Book for W. M. Evans. My labour was gratis, and after all the publisher made but poor use of it!

Oct. 10.—Heard old Mr. Williams, of Llanwrtyd; he did well at the great age of 91.

Dec. 3.—Wrote an article on "Pregethu" to *Seren Cymru.*

Dec. 18.—The "Fasting Girl" died at Pencader. She was supposed to have abstained from food for a long time. I never believed in her, though many did.

**1870.** Jan. 1.—Wrote an article for *Seren Cymru.*

Jan. 6.—My son Caleb went to Swansea to be apprenticed to the drapery.

Jan. 14.—Wrote a paper on Morgan John Rhys to *Seren Cymru.*

Jan. 25.—Wrote an article on "Hebraeg" for Mathetes' *Geiriadur.*

March 15, etc.—Wrote several letters to the *Daily Leader* on election matters.

May 17.—Wrote a paper to the *South Wales Press,* and again on 23rd.

May 28.—A leader to the *Carmarthen Weekly Reporter* on Gladstone. (See Collection.)

May 31.—Spoke at a public meeting on Sunday Closing.

June 4.—Am preparing sermons of Mr. Richards, Pontypridd, for the Press. (This vol. was finished at Cwmavon; price 6s.)

June 14 and 15.—At the Association at Kidwelly.

June 20.—Wrote a letter on "Confirmation" to the *Weekly Reporter.*

June 21.—The English Baptist Chapel was opened. Rev. Hugh Stowel Brown, of Liverpool, preached. He lectured the evening of the day following to a full audience at the Assembly Rooms. (See Collection of Newspaper Cuttings, pp. 15, 16, 17.)

June 24.—A letter to the *Reporter* on "Education."

July 5.—Translating the circular letter of the Brecon Association for W. Morgan Evans.

July 15.—The parents of the " Fasting Girl " were tried at the Assizes. Found guilty ; twelve months' imprisonment to the father and six months to the mother. They were farmers ; now ruined.

Aug. 16 and 17.—At the Bap. Union at Llanidloes.

Sep. 10.—Wrote the Rules of Old Ministers' Benefit Society for *Seren Cymru.*

Dec. 2.—Went to London to supply Castle Street Chapel for a month.

The following is an extract from my diary how I spent the month.

Dec. 3.—At the Bap. Mission House, the *Freeman* Office, Regent's Park Coll. 4th, Preached twice at Castle Street. Communion; good attendance. Heard Rev. Newman Hall at S. James's Hall at three p.m. 5th, Spent most of this dark, snowy day at the British Museum. 6th, Tea meeting and concert at Chapel. 7th, Went to St. Paul's Cathedral, Paternoster, Strand, etc. Heard Mr. Ll. Bevan at Whitfield's Chapel. 8th, With Dr. Underhill. Heard Dr. Parker at the Poultry ; very powerful. I preached at Castle Street. 9th, Went over to the Surrey side to see Mr. Spurgeon. Was with him some hours in the Tabernacle Vestry. 10th and 11th, In my study, at sermons and Esboniad. Preached twice on the Sunday. 12th, At proof of the Esboniad. In Hyde Park. At a concert by 600 or 700 singers in Exeter Hall. 13th, With Rev. Mr. Bevan at Whitfield's Tabernacle. Visited a sick member in Surrey. At a tea and public meeting at Paddington. 14th, At the Crystal Palace ; a world of wonders and music. 15th, Sat for my portrait in

Cheapside. Visited friends in Surrey. At Spurgeon's Tabernacle. Rev. James Spurgeon preached, and baptized 18. 16th, Study; wrote a long letter home. 17th, Very foggy. Went through the Houses of Parliament and Westminster Abbey. 18th, Preached twice; good meetings. At Bloomsbury Chapel at three. 19th, At the National Gallery. Visited Mrs. Evans in Surrey; near her death. Preached to a few Welsh at the Ragged School. 20th, Read proofs of Esboniad. Visited Mr. Owen Lewis at St. Pancras. Walked thence to the city. 21st, Cold and wintry. Took dinner and tea with Mr. Owen Lewis. Heard Dr. Landels. 22nd, Very snowy and slippery. Visited various places. Prayer meeting at Castle Street. 23rd, Study. At the rehearsal of Pencerdd Gwalia's Choir. 24th, At Chelsea. Visited Mr. Hy. Morgan. At S. Kensington Museum. 25th, Preached twice at Castle Street. Preached for the Welsh Independents at Hackney at three. 26th, Married Mr. David Thomas to Catherine Ann Davies, at Moorfields Chapel. Spent the day with the wedding party.

The Church at Castle Street gave me a unanimous "Call," offered me £100 a year to begin with, but I did not see my way to accept. (The "Call" and a Letter are on p. 39 of my Collection).

Dec. 27. Returned to Carmarthen. Found all well.

Vol. VI. contains 127 sermons, 416 pp.

**1871.** Jan. 1.—The same prayer. Preached twice. Communion.

Jan. 11.—Posted many letters to friends in order to get Mr. W. M. Lewis as Classical Tutor to Pontypool

College. I do my best for him, as he is a good young brother.

Jan. 24.—Wrote a long petition for our fishermen to the Secretary of State.

Feb. 6.—Committee at Pontypool. Mr. W. M. Lewis elected Classical Tutor.

March 22.—Removed to a new house in Francis Terrace.

April 12.—One of our members was buried at St. David's. An unworthy member, and a tippler; he ruined himself.

May 4 and 12.—Visited two prisoners at the gaol—one of them a Baptist!

May 15. — Temperance Conference at Swansea. Rev. Mr. Hughes, Tredegar, and myself preached at Dr. Rees' Chapel.

May 22 and 24.—At Pontypool College. Examined the Students in Greek, Hebrew, and Theology.

May 27.—Wrote a letter to the *S. W. Daily Press.* (Copy, p. 22.)

June 13 and 14.—At our Association at Aberystwyth.

June 18 and 19.—Rev. J. P. Chown, of Bradford, preached for the English Baptists. Very earnest and homely; good tendency.

June 20.—" Strolled round the town,
            With J. P. Chown."
He lectured for the English Baptists in the evening.

July 1.—A terrible accident occurred at the Nat. Prov. Bank this morning. The son of Mr. Victor, decorator, was assisting a workman to lower a ladder.

The rope used for lowering the ladder displaced some stone coping, which fell upon young Victor, killing him on the spot. I was passing, and saw it happen. It was an awful sight; so sudden. I feel deeply for the parents of this godly young man, who was much respected in the town.

July 5.—Heard Kilsby Jones preach at the Independent Chapel. He is a strange man ; don't know what to make of him !

July 31.—Finished the Old Testament, after seven years of patient labour. " I bless Thee, O God, for all Thy help." (I read all the Hebrew as I went along, and preached most of it on Sundays.)

Aug. 5.—Finished the " Appendix after Malachi." At Richards' sermons.

Aug. 21 and 23.—At the Baptist Union at Cefnmawr, N. Wales.

Sept. 27.—Translated " Pregeth gyntaf ac olaf y diacon " for *Seren Cymru.*

Oct. 10.—Wrote the history of Mrs. Statham. (Printed as a penny book.)

Oct. 17.—Wrote " Lefain." (This also printed as a penny book.)

Oct. 24.—We are now at war with the Church of England party *re* Education and our Elementary Schools. I wrote some letters to the Press on the question. (See Collection of Cuttings.)

Oct. 27.—A great public meeting was held at the Town Hall to transfer the Lancasterian Schools to the School Board. Tremendous row; meeting lasted until near midnight. We had the meeting with us, and got the victory. The subscribers' votes were 207 for, and only 51 against the transfer.

Dec. 6.—Began my Esboniad on the Acts; Rev. Mr. Roberts, of Pontypridd, did most of the four Gospels.

Dec. 31.—Preached twice. Communion in the evening. There is an Achan in the camp; may the Lord remove him! Amen. My work during this year on the Esboniad (Commentary) was hampered through the delay and subsequent failure of the publisher. This occurred in the middle of the Acts, and resulted in the stoppage of my work. It was finished Oct., 1888.

1872. Jan 15.—Visited Gellilednes, Peter Williams' old residence. The house much the same as in his time. (Wrote a paper on my visit, which appeared in *Seren Cymru.*)

Feb. 13 and 14.—Preached at the re-opening of Horeb, Cwmdwr; good meetings. Slept at Cym-yronen. (See Copy, p. 25.)

Feb. 24.—Wrote a letter to the *South Wales Daily News.*

March 8.—Wrote a letter to *Seren Cymru* about El Karey and his work in Palestine; another on 30th.

March 28.—Heard the eminent Ieuan Gwyllt lecture on "Psalmody" at Water Street Chapel. Excellent.

April 12. — Read a proof of my "Pwnc" on "Iachawdwriaeth" (Salvation). It is rather long, but it will do.

April 27.—Finished my paper on "Wine" for the Conference of the Temperance Association at Merthyr Tydfil. (Copy, pp. 27-31.)

May 16.—"Gwilym Mai," our Bard, died suddenly
last night. He was a very faithful member of the
Church at Lammas Street.

June 28-30.—At the Temperance Association.
Large crowds attended the meetings.

July 11 and 12.—At our Association at Ferryside.
Fairly good.

July 14.—These sermons of Mr. Richards, Pontypridd, were written by him for delivery as discourses,
and not for reading. I rearranged the matter for
publication in a serial form. Preparing Sermon No.
19 of Mr. Richards for the Press; re-wrote it all.
(See Copy, p. 32.)

July 16. — My dear little daughter Bessie, our
youngest child, died at 10.15 a.m. She was taken ill
with typhoid fever on the previous day.

July 18.—We buried our dear Mary Elizabeth at the
Cemetery. Rev. Mr. Lewis (Homo Ddu) officiated at
the funeral. He also preached in my stead on the
Thursday evening. This has been a severe blow to
me and my wife—little Bessie was such an affectionate
child. Now she has gone to join her dear sister in
the world of joy. I shall have two angels in heaven
now. Will they know each other? O blessed meeting! I see them smile together, and walk arm in arm
in beauty and whiteness and joy up to the very Throne
of the Lamb. "O, my God, help me and help my wife.
And O! bless the other six children, and bring them
safe to the place where part of the family is already
gathered."

Aug. 5.—Took my family for a fortnight to Ferryside to the sea. My son Tom, being in a situation at

Merthyr, caught small-pox. Was in hospital there for a few weeks. I went to see him as soon as the authorities allowed, and found him recovering. Very much comforted.

Aug. 21.—At the Baptist Union at Swansea. Read a short paper.

Sept. 3.—Heard two fine sermons at Lammas Street Chapel by Dr. T. Rees and Thomas, Bangor.

Sept. 13.—At the funeral of Rev. J. Morris, the minister at Cwmifor.

Sept. 17.—At the Ordination of Mr. Lewis Davies, Plashet.

Oct. 7.—At the Baptist Union at Manchester; the best thing there was Mr. Spurgeon's Address at the Free Trade Hall.

Nov. 24.—Preached at my old church, Llanthewy.. Communion.

Dec. 8.—Have been unwell for some time; preached in the morning only. Great storm at night—the earth seemed to shake.

This year has been remarkable for rain and storms. Have done but little work since the death of my dear little girl; that put me out of the working spirit, and am unable to return.

1873.—" O, my God, be with me, and bless me this year! "

Jan. 7.—Wrote an article to *Seren Cymru* on " Pa le mae'r bai? "

Feb. 6.—At the funeral of James Williams, a tin-worker; he was a hard drinker, and died at middle age. When a publican visited his death-bed, he cursed him, and ordered him from the room. Another —a public-house woman, where he used to drink, called, but he said to her, " You have put nails into my coffin; go out of my sight!" He had some religious feeling when in health. His wife was a member; he went at times to the English Baptist Chapel, as he understood but little Welsh.

Feb. 14.—Coal has gone up to 31s. 8d. a ton ; it has doubled in price.

Feb. 18.—A Good Templar's Lodge was opened, which I joined, though I did not like its pomp and cost.

April 18.—At Abergavenny. Mrs. Davies (wife of Mr. Davies, ironmonger, of Pontypool) was buried at Llanwenarth. Her funeral over, we returned and buried her sister, Mrs. Fox, of Abergavenny (my wife's mother), at Froginore Street burial ground. A strange coincidence that the sisters should both be buried at the same time—Mrs. Fox, 75 ; Mrs. Davies, 67.

May 26.—Sent a letter to the *South Wales Press* (see copy 37, 38).

May 27 and 28. The Temperance Association was held in our town; as chairman I delivered an address, which was printed.

June 1.—Rev. H. W. Jones, of the Tabernacle, died this morning. He was a popular speaker at public meetings. His age was 72.

June 10 and 11.—An Association was held at Cwmdwr —my mother church—at which I preached ; never held here before.

July 9.—I reviewed Rev. A. J. Parry's "Meat Argument" for *Seren Cymru.*

Aug. 1.—Wrote "Esgob Winchester" for *Seren Cymru.*

Sept. 9.—Wrote a short letter to the *Weekly Reporter.*

Sept. 16.—Have finished my Exposition on the Acts.

Oct. 2.—Wrote a letter to *Seren Cymru* on what appeared in the *Haul.*

Oct. 7 and 8.—At special meetings at Ebenezer, Llangunog; Dr. Davies (the blind man) and myself were the preachers. Though the doctor was much broken, he did well. I had a lengthy talk with him about the death of Christmas Evans, at Swansea. I wanted to get all the information I could, as I thought it probable I might never see him again—and so it proved. The doctor said, "that as Christmas Evans died at his house, he ought to know something of his state of mind when his end had come. Christmas Evans was never more popular and effective than on his last preaching tour. He was likewise more heavenly in his spirit; he seemed to be at peace with all his old acquaintances left behind. His last affliction was both light and short; he did not at first think that he would die of that illness; but when he felt and believed that his death was at hand, he was suddenly filled with perfect peace. Dr. Davies thought that there was no happier man on earth than was Christmas Evans in the prospect of death."

Nov. 5.—Heard Revs. S. Roberts, Llanbrynmair, and Lewis, of Henllan, preach at Lammas Street Chapel. Mr. Roberts was full of wit, but Mr. Lewis was heavy though very able. Heard also Revs. Michael Jones, of Bala, and Thomas of Bangor.

Nov. 10.—Old John Davies (our oldest member but one, Thomas Davies, his brother, being 98) died, aged 90—the age on coffin plate was 94; am not sure which is correct. He was a member when I settled here; and I never knew a better Christian. He was full of love to Christ and religion. He had great power and freedom in prayer; he was always present at our meetings; it was to me a great pleasure to see him at the end of the platform listening to the preaching; his smiles and glowing face often cheered me. At the last Communion he had on the Sunday night before his death he was unusually joyous; he sang at the close of the Ordinance as if he were in sight of Heaven. He repeated the hymn several times (in Welsh, of course)—

" Hallelujah ! praise to Jesus for His Grace on Calvary," etc.

His like is not left in the chapel. Though a pauper, he often made me feel rich. I am afraid his grave has been covered by the new Vestry.

Nov. 18.—Wrote an article on Good Templary to *Seren Cymru*; also another on the 21st inst., and also on December 12th.

Dec. 25 (Xmas).—Mr. David Lewis, a member with the English Baptists, was Mayor this year. It was the custom to attend service in state at St. Peter's on this day; but Mr. Lewis consistently refused, and attended his chapel instead. At this, some churchmen were very angry—even threatened to fine him !

1874.—Here I begin another year. "O, my God, keep me from all sin, and help me by Thy Spirit, for Christ's sake. Amen."

Jan. 2.—Wrote an article on Good Templary for *Seren Cymru*.

Jan. 4.—Very unwell. Though under medical treatment, I had to preach four times—twice at home, once at the English Baptist Church, and once at the Union. Much time has been given to the election of an M.P. (see collection pp. 88, 89).

Feb. 11.—Went to Caerphilly to record my vote for Talbot.

March 3.—Wrote a letter to the *Carmarthen Weekly Reporter* (see collection).

March 18.—Spoke at the Town Hall, when we collected for the Bengal famine fund, Bishop Thirlwall in the chair. I had a chat with him in Welsh—a nice old gentleman.

March 22.—Communion; dedicated our new Communion plate.

April 15.—Planted an evergreen on the grave of dear Bessie.

April 21.—At a recognition service at Lammas Street Chapel; good meetings. Sent a full account to *Carmarthen Express*.

April 26.—Preached at the Tabernacle in morning, and at home in the evening; large congregations. I have now finished here.

April 27.—The Mayor presided over a very large meeting in chapel to present me with a testimonial on my leaving. It consisted of a handsomely-engraved gold watch, and a purse of £11 14s. The proceedings were fully reported in the daily and local press, cuttings from which I have framed.

During my eleven years at Carmarthen these were the church figures:—Baptized, 169; restored, 62; received by letters, 168. Total, 399. Died, 105; dismissed, 173; expelled, 74. Total, 352. Number of members when I left, 339. I kept the church book, and left it in perfect order at the date of my exit. Vol. VIII. contains my sermons to the end of my ministry at Carmarthen; number 155, and cover, 650 pp.

## RISCA (MON.).

April 29.—Left Carmarthen, and arrived at Risca in the afternoon without any mishap. We can never be thankful enough to the Lord for all His kindness.

May 3.—Began my ministry at Moriah, Risca; my salary here was the same as at Carmarthen.

May 19 and 20.—At the annual meetings of Pontypool College.

May 26 and 27.—At the Association at Hermon, Nantyglo. Began well, but the stage fell at 10 a.m. when I was just beginning to preach. One old woman was killed, and another injured; many others had narrow escapes. Of course the meetings were no good after this sad occurrence.

July 16.—Site for my new house was marked out. I built a neat dwelling called "Greenland House," which cost me £300. After occupying it for more than eleven years I sold it for £245.

Sep. 9.—Began to write an article on Richards, Pontypridd, to the *Gwyddoniadur.* Mr. Gee paid (I think) £2 for it.

Dec. 4.—Election of Risca School Board. There was a sharp contest—six for five seats. Mr. Edwards, grocer, came in first, and I second, on the list. I was a member of the Board six years, and Clerk three years. (See Copy, page 42.)

Never in my life had I more Meetings and Committees of all sorts to attend, and fewer hours to myself of quiet. Building a new house taxed me heavily. Preaching and meetings at Cwmynant—a branch of Moriah—added much to my work. This appears to me a strange sphere.

**1875.** March 10 to 15.—Removed into our new house. " May the Lord bless our dwelling. Amen."

May 18 and 19.—At the annual meetings of the Pontypool College.

May 25 and 26.—At the Association at Llaniddel.

June 8.—At the ordination of Mr. Maurice at Tirzah.

July 14.—Went to the Temperance Association at Aberdare.

July 15.—Very heavy rain and storm. The pond at Cwmcarn burst, and the flood rushed down from Cross Keys to Risca with terrific force. The canal and the turnpike road were cut through, and the waters of the canal joined the flood. John Hunt's factory was destroyed, his house swept away, and the family of eleven perished. Another house near, inhabited by Howell Davies, his son and daughter, was also swept away, and all three perished. The body of Howell

Davies was never found. Risca and Pontymister were flooded. Water in most of the houses, gardens spoiled, roads torn up. It will take hundreds of pounds to repair the immense damage. All this happened at midnight. John Hunt, his wife, two sons, two daughters, and an apprentice were all buried the same day (Sunday). On the Monday the son and daughter of Howell Davies were buried. Howell Davies was a Calv. Methodist, and a godly man. Hunt was a Free-thinker. The scene from the pond to the bridge below the factory was awful. The same night a waterspout tore up the field by the old copper works and caused much loss and damage.

July 26.—Examining the papers of Llangollen College Students.

Oct. 10.—Dedicated our new Communion service of plate.

Oct. 20 and 21.—Temperance Conference at Swansea. I was appointed to write an address to be sent to all the Churches and Chapels in Wales. It was signed by one minister of every denomination—the Rector of Neath (Rev. Griffiths) for the Established Church.

Dec. 17.—The monument of Rev. D. R. Stephen was unveiled at Newport Old Cemetery. It was an imposing affair.

This was a year of very hard work—at such a variety of things. Rev. Mr. Thomas, of Bethany, Risca, and myself held many preaching services at Newtown (North Risca) on the afternoons of Sundays, both indoors and open air. We intended to put up a

Chapel there. We baptized a few; but at last the majority decided to build at Cross Keys.

**1876.** March 5.—Went early to Abergavenny to bury my wife's father, Mr. Charles Fox. We buried him on the Wednesday at the Cemetery; his age was 78. Both Mr. and Mrs. Fox were old members at Frogmore Street Chapel.

April 26.—At Abercarn. Preached at Mr. Probert's Chapel. After this I had a severe pain in the left side of my brain. Was unable to do anything for several days.

May 21.—My dear friend, Mr. David Lewis, merchant, of Carmarthen (he was Mayor when I left), died, aged 45. He was buried at the Cemetery. He was a member at Priory Street Chapel till 1868, when the English Church was formed. Ever ready to help in every way. He was very kind to me and my family; was exceedingly good to the poor. Though feeble in health he was an active Christian. How I feel at the thought of never seeing him again in this world. His epitaph is :—

"Until the day break and the shadows flee away."
In affectionate remembrance of
DAVID LEWIS, Merchant, Carmarthen.
Died May 21st, 1876, aged 45 years.
"Blessed are the merciful, for they shall obtain mercy."

May 24.—At the annual meetings of Pontypool College.

May 30 and 31.—At our Association at Beaufort; poor meetings.

Aug. 17.—A rare meeting to-day. All my living children—six in number—are here to-day; the other two are in heaven. It is very seldom that we thus meet !

May 29.—Went to Talgarth; visited old Trevecca. Had an hour with Prof. Howells. He showed me books, MSS., guns, the relics of Howel Harris. All very interesting to me.

Sept. 6.—A good day's work. Went to Llangammarch, Llandovery, Cwmyronen, Ffosywhiaid, Trelath, and at Llanwrtyd by 9 p.m. I travelled over 30 miles this day, and witnessed the scenes of my childhood.

Sept. 20.—Went to Cardiff to the presentation of Dr. Thomas, late Pontypool Tutor. It was a brilliant affair. The Doctor received 2,000 guineas and an address. Sir Robert Lush presided at the function.

Oct. 30.—At the unveiling of Nefydd's Monument at Old Blaenau.

Nov. 15.—At the funeral of Rev. S. Williams, Hermon, Nantyglo. 18th, Sent a letter to the *Seren Cymru.*

Dec. 31.—Preached twice; good meetings; Communion. Here ends another year, the best of my life as regards worldly matters. We had much help from the estate of Mr. and Mrs. Fox.

**1877.** This year, like the rest, has been full of work. (See Diary.)

April 5.—Delivered a lecture at Moriah Chapel on " Welsh Reformers," Mr. Evans, of Cefn, in the chair. Successful.

April 20 and May 10.—Wrote letters on both dates for *Seren Cymru.*

May 22 and 23.—At the annual meetings of the Pontypool College. A stormy election of President. Mr. W. M. Lewis was chosen by 81 votes, against 51 for Mr. Williams, of Merthyr. Dd. Thomas was elected Classical Tutor unopposed.

May 29 and 30.—At our Association at Castleton.

July 10.—Wrote an article on "Deacons." 20th, another; and on 28th, another on "Tithes." All in the *Seren Cymru.*

Aug. 15 and 16.—At the Baptist Union at Elim, Penydarren; passed well.

Oct. 9 to 11.—At the Autumnal Session of the Baptist Union of Great Britain and Ireland at Newport; large attendances.

This year has been a memorable one throughout. Trade bad everywhere; thousands have seen want; the tin works at Pontymister stopped; my salary came down from £8 to £3 or £4 per month. I fear the people took advantage of the little private means we had. A large number have died of famine in India. A fearful war was going on between Russia and Turkey. Religion in our country has been very low throughout the year.

1878.—This year begins in gloom, yet I and mine suffer no want.

Jan. 25.—Sent a sermon of Rev. Richards, Pontypridd, to *Seren Cymru.*

Feb. 6.—The Vicar and myself visited those in distress in order to help them. We had a large Relief Committee.

Jan. 9.—These are dire times; great poverty still in South Wales, and other places. Many who sinfully rolled in luxury, now depend on charity. Our Parliament is in a whirlwind; we are on the eve of war. The Turks are conquered, the Russians are at Constantinople, and the English are in fear of their "Interests." In the midst of all this the "infallible" Pius IX. died, aged 85. Glad would I be if the last Pope had gone. May the Lord pity our miserable world, and bring order out of chaos!

Feb. 23.—Corrected the last proof of Mr. Richards' sermons, which I began about seven years ago.

March 1.—Lent the "Book of Spirites," by Edmund Jones, to the Bard Islwyn. (He died soon after, and the book is lost.)

May 21 and 22.—At the annual meetings of Pontypool College.

May 28 and 29.—At our Association at Rhymney.

June 3.—I have now ready a shilling book of Rev. Titus Lewis' sermons. I found his MSS. at Carmarthen (printed by Mr. William Jones, Newport). The book contains twenty-seven sermons, and an account of his life-work. I went to Pembrokeshire Association, at St. Dogmell's, and Carmarthenshire Association, at Cwmifor, and sold nearly the whole.

July 16 (and following days).—Visited Bristol, Chepstow, Tintern, Monmouth, with my wife and two children.

Sept. 11.—The terrible colliery explosion at Abercarn. I was at Cardiff preaching, and returned to Newport on hearing the news, and proceeded to

Abercarn. Two hundred and fifty-eight colliers have perished, 246 of whom were never brought to bank. The pit was closed for a considerable time. Oh! the destruction and misery—the dire penalty of coal mining.

Nov. 21.—Wrote to the *Seren Cymru* on my tour in Pembrokeshire.

Nov. 27.—At the funeral of "Islwyn"; buried at Babell; many present. Great poverty; calamities and misery characterised this year, yet through all God has favoured me and mine. I had immense difficulty in carrying on the work of the School Board. Vol. I. of English sermons from 1874 to 1878 ; they number 220, occupying 1,022 pp.

1879. Jan. 2.—At Pontypool College Committee. I went up to Ebenezer, the chapel where the Rev. Edmund Jones (of ghostly memory) is buried. There is in the chapel a large tablet with this epitaph : " In this yard are deposited the remains of the Rev. Edmund Jones, late minister of this church, who was faithful in Christ's vineyard for 70 years. He died Nov. 26th, 1793, aged 91 years and 7 months. He also erected this house, and settled it for the use of the Independent Religious Society here assembled till time shall be no more."

Feb. 10.—Went to Blaenavon to the funeral of my dear brother and fellow-student, Rev. Dl. Morgan. A very large attendance.

March 4.—Went to meet the School Board auditor at Newport. Here I may state, that owing to mistakes in the books when handed to me by the previous clerk, I had no end of trouble for many weeks. We found out at last that he owed the Board more than £69, which he paid after being allowed grace.

March 17.—A Thanksgiving Meeting was held in all the chapels on account of the re-starting of the Tin Works, which had been idle more than two years. Oh! the poverty here during that long time.

May 21.—At the annual meetings of Pontypool College. I wrote an account of the proceedings to the *Seren Cymru.*

May 27 and 28.—At the Association at Beulah; meetings most miserable, as weather was bad all through.

July 25.—Went to London; preached twice at Castle Street Chapel on the Sunday; weather very hot.

July 29.—Went to Bedford and to Elstow—the old home of John Bunyan. Saw very many curiosities. Bought many photographs bearing on him, and copied many old records (see end of my diary). Went to Olney, to Hackleton, back to St. Alban's, and London.

July 31.—Spent several hours at the Doré Gallery —the great picture was "Christ leaving the Prætorium."

Aug. 7.—I bade farewell once more to London, and returned home.

Aug. 14.—Sent an account of my Bedfordshire tour to *Seren Cymru.*

Oct. 2.—Appeared before the Revising Barrister to defend my vote, as the Tories had objected; they had to pay my expenses—10s.

Oct. 23.— Began my Welsh Article on "The Ministry," for the quarterly *Seren Gomer.*

Nov. 12.—Copied a sermon of Mr. Richards, Pontypridd, for the *Greal.*

Nov. 19 and 20.—At Sunday Closing Meetings at Swansea; heard a speech from Mr. Henry Richard, M.P.

Dec. 28. — Communion; very bad weather; few present.

Dec. 28 and 29.—We heard awful news from Dundee: during the storm on Sunday night the Tay Bridge was blown down, and a train passing over the Firth was buried in the boiling surf, and every passenger —supposed to have been about 100—perished in the waters.

**1880.** April 17. — Being the Moderator of our Association this year, I now begin to prepare the " Address from the Chair," which will be the Circular Letter. The subject is " Things to be considered."

May 18 and 19.—At the annual meetings of Pontypool College.

May 26 and 27.—At the Association at Tredegar. All went well; but the weather was rough and showery.

May 30.—Preached twice; finished my ministry at Moriah; no co-operation in the church; salary was very low for a long time; the leaders were men of straw, and I had altogether a rather unhappy pastorate, because I insisted on doing what was right. Subsequent events proved my actions to have been wise and just, and retribution followed those who

K

caused the unpleasantness and harm to religion. During my ministry of six years at Moriah, I baptized 39 persons. I determined not to take another church; I was clerk to the School Board. I had built my own house, so it was not convenient to remove; and I resolved to continue preaching as long as I was able, and whenever I might be wanted.

I worked very hard while at Risca. As Pastor, I attended Bible Classes, Singing Schools, Y.M.C.A.'s, Temperance Meetings, Political Meetings, and School Board Meetings without number. During my School Board clerkship, a new school was built at Pontymister; the old school at Risca was enlarged, and a new school built at Cross Keys. I wrote several hundred letters to the Education Department, and to other parties. More than £7,000 passed through my accounts, and without one shilling error. Sermons, Vol. II., pp. 179, contains all to the end of my pastorate at Moriah, and number 63. "My God, I thank Thee for all help. Amen."

June 4.—Went to London. Preached (6th) twice at Castle Street, and baptized one. 7th, At Dr. Williams' Library. 9th, At the Welsh Liberal Demonstration at the Crystal Palace. 10th, At the Liberation Society's Conference, Cannon Street Hotel; two sittings. There I saw Mr. Miall last; he was too poorly to speak, but stood up, and was cheered immensely. 11th, At a Liberation meeting at Spurgeon's Tabernacle. 13th, Preached again at Castle Street Chapel. 15th, At the Education Department. 17th, At the prayer meeting at Castle Street. 20th, Preached twice at Castle

Street. 22nd, At Mr. Spurgeon's Orphanages ; the foundation stones of six houses were laid. 25th, At City Road Chapel ; heard Rev. Morley Punshon preach. He was not up to what I had heard from him before. (He died shortly after this date.) 27th, Preached twice at Castle Street.

June 29.—At the Sunday School Centenary Conference at the Memorial Hall. Heard men of many nations speak, some of whom had but very little English.

June 30.—At the Sunday School Centenary. Great Demonstration, Crystal Palace—100,000 people present ; 70,000 of them were Sunday School children. The singing was grand !

July 1.—Left London for home. Safe in port at 7 p.m. *Laus Deo.*

July 4.—Preached twice at Crane Street Chapel, Pontypool.

July 11.—An idle Sunday for me ; did not preach. I and my wife went to the Cefn, to which church we have transferred.

July 15.—A dreadful explosion took place at Risca pit ; 120 men, and 69 horses were killed. The last bodies were not found until four months after the accident !

July 18.—Preached twice at Crane Street Chapel, Pontypool.

July 25.—At Sunday School Anniversary at Henllys. Tea Meeting following day.

Aug. 7.—Wrote an article to the *Greal*—" Y pwys o ferthin Crefydd personol " (The importance of cultivating personal religion).

Aug. 9-12.—At the Baptist Union Meetings at Cardiff. Sent an account to the *Seren Cymru.*

I acted as deputy-tutor at Pontypool College for three months, Professor Lewis being ill from home.

Oct. 19.—Heard of the death of Mr. Lewis in Switzerland. His body was brought home, and buried at Carmarthen, his native place. At his funeral at Carmarthen, Oct. 25th.

Nov. 13.—Went to Berkeley, Glos., a small old town. The Church and the Castle are very interesting. Went thence to Nailsworth, and preached on the Sunday at Shortwood, Benjamin Francis's old church. At Nailsworth in the evening; also on the Monday evening. Tuesday I preached thrice. I had longed to see this old place. I had great kindness shown me, and a gift of £3.

Nov. 19.—Wrote an article on Benjamin Francis to *Seren Cymru.*

Dec. 21.—Attended before the Commissioners for Higher Education in Wales at Newport (see press copy, p. 47).

Dec. 27.—Began to write about H. H. Williams to *Seren Gomer.* During this year I wrote some of "The History of the Baptists" in this county. I intend to publish our history, if sufficiently encouraged to proceed with the work.

1881. Feb. 19.—Transcribed one of Mr. Richards' sermons for the *Greal.*

March 19.—On the examination papers of Llangollen students

April 17 and 18.—At the annual meetings of Pontypool College.

April 19.—Lord Beaconsfield died this morning, aged 76. It is astonishing how much is made of him in the newspapers. His last words were, " I am overwhelmed." What could he mean? This obscurity is in keeping with his whole life. Had he died five or ten years before, the world would have been happier, and, perhaps, saved from some war! I have commenced a register, or short account, of all the deceased students from the opening of the college at Abergavenny till now. This will be an extensive task; it is not to be printed, but kept in the college for reference.

May 8.—At the Cefn Church. I did not have it smooth at Moriah—poor Evans has it far rougher here!

May 24 and 25.—At our Association at Nebo—a happy one. Dr. Jones, of Llangollen, preached most admirably; he was at my house from the Monday till Tuesday, and we went together to Nebo. How I loved him! Alas! he is gone. Active and useful to the utmost was he.

July 2.—The American President, Garfield, was shot by Guiteau, and died on Sept. 20th. He was in his prime—only 50. His ancestors left England in the time of the Puritan persecution. Garfield's mother descended from the Huguenots of France. He was an excellent man—a Christian, and a Baptist. His awful death has filled millions with horror.

Aug. 10 and 11.—At the Baptist Union meetings at Treorky.

Sept. 4.—At Olchon—no chapel there.  Preached at a farm-house—Bailie Bach, at 2 p.m., and at another farm—Black Pill, at 6.  It is an out of the way dingle, very convenient to our fathers in time of persecution.

Nov. 11.—At Pontypool College.  The students have shown disobedience to the Committee ; 18 of them left the college, but they soon repented and returned.  Peace was soon restored, and no harm was done.  I sent an account of the mutiny to the *Seren Cymru.*

Dec. 12.—At the funeral of Dr. Thomas, at Penygarn —my dear old tutor.  We were true friends, and I feel deeply after him.

I preached about 50 times during this year, and delivered many addresses in churches on Baptist History.

**1882.**  Jan. 29.—Wrote a sermon (*Psa.* cxli. 8) of Mr. Richards' to *Greal.*  Preached in the evening at Bethany, Risca.

March 22.—On the examination papers of Llangollen students.

April 27.—Wrote a paper to *Seren Cymru.*

June 24.—Wrote an account of Tintern Abbey to *Seren Cymru.*

Aug. 20.—Preached for the third time at Tintern ; a very heathenish place.  We have formed here a Baptist church.  A full account appeared in the *Baptist,* written by Mr. Mayo, of Chepstow.

Sept. 5.—Preparing a paper for the Baptist Union meetings (Llandudno).

Sept. 20.—Went to Newport to hear Moody and Sankey.  Of the two, Sankey, the Singer, was the best.

Oct. 9-11.—At the Baptist Union meetings at Llandudno; stayed a night at Leominster; examined some MSS. of the excellent Joshua Thomas, the Baptist historian; borrowed two of his volumes; saw his grave. Subsequently I wrote a long article to the *Seren Gomer*. Having been appointed at Llandudno to edit the *Baptist Handbook*, I began now to prepare it for next year.

Much of this year was occupied in School Board work, and writing the "History of the Baptists in Monmouthshire." I preached about 70 times. "Hitherto hath the Lord helped me."

One of the most horrible events of the year was the assassination of Cavendish and Burke in Phœnix Park, Dublin, on April 19th (see notes at end of diary).

**1883.**—Mr. Leon Gambetta, the great French Republican, died with the old year—at midnight, aged 45. His death resulted from blood-poisoning, caused by his accidentally discharging a pistol, and wounding himself in the hand. His suffering for four hours before death was most intense. As he was a Materialist, he had no religious consolation, and his last words were awful—"I am lost; it is useless to disguise it, but I have suffered so much that it will be a relief." This account was written by the *Times* Paris correspondent.

I had severe cold at the beginning of this year; it terminated in bronchitis, from which I never thoroughly recovered. I continued my ordinary work through it all, but often failed to preach owing to cough. For a while I was afflicted with deafness, and head noises.

July 18.—Went away in search of health for a time —to Carmarthen, Llanstephan, and on the hills of Swyddffynon—beneficially.

Sept. 9.—Prepared a sermon of Mr. Richards' for the *Greal.*

During this year I preached about 60 times—often with difficulty. Much time devoted to the *Handbook.*

**1884.** Jan. 6.—Prepared a sermon of Mr. Richards' (*Amos* v. 8), and 21st, Another; both for the *Greal.* 23rd, Wrote for the *South Wales Daily News.*

Feb. 2.—Prepared a paper on " The Union of Wales with England," for the *Geninen.*

Feb. 27.—A paper for the *Seren Cymru* on " The Arrogance of Churchism."

May 1.—Went to Newport with my youngest son, Percy, who was determined to go to sea. He made one voyage of 13 months; then came back. After a time in the grocery and drapery, he went to sea again.

Nov. 9-20.—Went to North Wales; attended two Associations, at Denbigh and Carnarvon. Preached in many places before returning home.

Aug. 11.—Went to Holyhead to the Baptist Union meetings : excellent.

Aug. 15.—Went across to Ireland ; spent a day in Kingstown and Dublin. Had a rough passage, but returned home safely.

Sept. 4.—Preparing a short memoir of my cousin, Rev. Rees Evans, for the *Greal.* Sent a sermon of Mr. Richards' to the same periodical

Oct. 22,—Baptist Union meetings at Llanidloes; good meetings.

Dec. 8.—Am writing an article on the Papacy to *Seren Gomer.*

Between this and the end of the year, I dispatched by post and rail 4,000 copies of the *Handbook.* Payment slow coming.

Xmas Day.—An earthquake was felt and heard in Spain. It lasted, with few intervals, for several days; thousands perished. The poor deluded Catholics rushed into the streets, and carried out their images from the churches, in order, if possible, to excite their commiseration. Oh! Popery.

During this year now ending I preached about 60 times.

**1885.** Jan. 23 and 30.—Wrote letters to the *Seren Cymru.*

Feb. 26.—Wrote the history of Beulah Church to *Seren Cymru.*

May 19.—At the annual meetings of Pontypool College.

May 26 and 27.—At our Association at Pontypool. Began my paper on the Revised Version. (These were printed and sold for 2d. each.)

June 7.—Went to Breconshire; preached at Llangorse on Sunday; went to the Brecon Association—poor meetings. Went to Llanfyrnach to see my old aunt (my mother's sister); very aged, but wonderfully well; home on 10th.

July 14.—Began my paper on Monmouthshire for the *Geninen*; the payment I get in return is the *Geninen* quarterly.

Aug. 4.—Sent memoirs of deceased ministers in Wales to Mr. Booth for the *Baptist Handbook.*

Aug. 6.—Began my reply on Baptism to Idrisyn Jones, of Newport. (The edition of 2,000 was soon sold at 2d. each.)

Aug. 11 and 12.—At the Baptist Union at St. Dogmell's—excellent.

Aug. 22.—Wrote an account to the *Seren Cymru.*

Sept. 14-16.—At the Temperance Jubilee at Merthyr; two addresses; Dr. J. Thomas, Liverpool, and Rev. T. Levi with me.

Nov. 30.—Election day—much time spent for weeks previously on this.

Dec. 2.—Went to Caerphilly to vote for Mr. Alfred Thomas.

Dec. 15.—Wrote a short account of Morgan John Rhys to the *Monmouthshire Baptist.* I preached about 55 times this year; and here end another 12 months. I have no reason to complain, but rather to say—" Blessed be the Lord for all His mercies, and constant goodness. Pardon Thou all my sins, for Christ's sake." I should like to preach more, but I feel silence and rest both necessary.

1886.—Here begins another year. " To Thee alone I look, and in Thee I trust."

Jan. 15.—The *Santa Clara,* an American ship, struck the steamer, *Admiral Morson,* near Holyhead; several lost their lives, and Captain Weeks perished. I knew him—his wife was the daughter of my cousin, Rev. R. Evans.

Jan. 24.—The Fenians have blown up a part of the House of Commons and the Tower—awful! Some lives have been sacrificed. May Heaven defeat these servants of the devil!

Feb. 4.—Wrote a letter to the *Seren Cymru.*

Feb. 16.—Began to write the history of Blaenau Gwent Church for *Seren Gomer.*

Feb. 27.—Dispatched examination papers to Llangollen students.

March 13.—Wrote a letter to the *Seren Cymru.*

March 22.—At Carmarthen, burying Mary Vaughan, aged 34. I baptized her; she was a pious young woman, a zealous member, and a devoted Sunday scholar and teacher.

March 27.—Wrote for the *Seren Cymru.* April 20th, On Ireland, to same paper.

April 28.—Dr. Rees, of Swansea, died in his 70th year. Knew him well—a great man and most pathetic preacher. I grieve that I shall never hear him again. Only the previous week, Rev. Simon Evans, of Hebron, died. I knew him also. Thus the Independents have lost two of their best men in South Wales.

May 5.—Brinley Richards passed away. All Wales mourns after her great musician. How many Welshmen have to thank him!

May 18 and 19.—At the annual meetings of Pontypool College.

May 25 and 26.—At our Association at Abercarn; this was rather poor, as the weather was unfavourable.

May 29.—Wrote a paper, "The History of our Colleges," for the *Monmouthshire Baptist.*

June 18.—Wrote for the *Seren Cymru.*

July 1 and 2.—Having made a sale of part of our furniture, and sold our house to Bethany Church as a minister's residence, we removed to Newport. Having now no pastorate, we found it would be more convenient living in town than at Pontymister.

July 9.—Most part of the University College at Aberystwyth was burnt; and, sad to say, some men lost their lives. The damage was great, and the loss is estimated at £30,000.

Aug. 10-12.—At the Baptist Union at Gadlys, Aberdare, which passed exceedingly well.

Aug. 19.—Wrote a paper on " Llanvaches " to the *Monmouthshire Baptist.*

Sept. 10.—Preparing a short paper for the Jubilee of Pontypool College.

Sept. 13.—Sent some Welsh Memoirs to Mr. Booth for *Baptist Handbook,* 1887.

Sept. 16.—Wrote " A Cry from the Past " to the *Seren Cymru.*

Sept. 17.—A few ministers (including myself) had half-an-hour with the celebrated Rev. Henry Ward Beecher at the Westgate Hotel. In the evening, at the Albert Hall, he lectured on " The Wastes and Burdens of Society." He was more interesting in conversation than as a lecturer. A first-rate talker, but spoke too low for the audience. He was rather short and stout in person ; he looked well. His wife, who was with him, looked aged and tired. Mr. Beecher died shortly after his return to America.

Sept. 29-30.—At the Jubilee of Pontypool College; Rev. E. Edwards, of Torquay, preached a masterly sermon. I read a paper on the "History of the College." It was translated for the *Seren Cymru*, and appeared in October.

Oct. 21.—Heard the eminent traveller, H. M. Stanley, at the Albert Hall. There was a full audience. The lecture was read, and was rather tame; many were disappointed. Mr. Stanley's forte is not the platform; he looked pale, delicate, and quiet. He went soon after to explore Africa.

November.—I dispatched 4,000 Welsh Diaries. (I was editor.)

Dec. 7.—Wrote a short letter for the memoir of Rev. T. Williams, of Ebenezer, Llangynog—published by his son.

Dec. 10.—Terrible reports of storms and wrecks at sea.

Dec. 18.—Wrote Sunday School lessons for the *Seren Cymru.*

Dec. 26.—Preached at Tirzah—heavy snow. Walked to Rhiwderin after the evening service, and was nearly stopped by the driving snow; but I was helped and saved!

Dec. 27.—At an Eisteddfod at the Albert Hall. Sir George Elliott, the expected chairman, did not come; I had to take his place. I considered it small honor; my friends thought otherwise!

I preached on 26 Sundays during this year.

**1887.** Jan. 1.—"I pray for Thy favor, O God, this year."

Jan. 18.—Finished my last Sunday School lesson for *Seren Cymru*.

Jan. 31.—Attended the Ordination of Mr. Rees at Cwmbran.

Feb. 5.—Transcribed a sermon of Rev. James Richards', of Pontypridd, for the *Greal*. Several appeared from time to time.

Feb. 14.—Rev. Timothy Thomas died last night, aged 76; he had been an eminent minister at Cefn and other places.

April 4.—Wrote a letter to *Seren Cymru, re* an article in the *Geninen*.

April 30.—Wrote a letter on certain hymns to *Banner and Times of Wales*.

May 7.—Wrote a short paper on " Blaenyglyn " to *Seren Cymru*.

May 11.—Re-commenced my Commentary on the New Testament; it stopped at Carmarthen, at the 19th chapter of *Acts*, but the MS. was ready to the end of that book. To-day I began *Romans*. Four-and-a-half parts appeared during the subsequent months, and the work was finished. Mr. David Davies, of Merthyr, gave me material help to pay Mr. Jones, of Newport, the printer, to whom I paid £137. I repaid Mr. Davies all the money lent.

May 30.—At the Centenary of Sunday Schools at Hengoed; read a paper on Morgan John Rhys, which appeared in the *Seren Cymru*.

June 3.—Having gone through *Romans* once, I now revise for press.

June 7.—Had the gratification of hearing Mr. Gladstone, at the Albert Hall, at noon. Crowds filled the streets, and the enthusiasm of the people was indescribable.

June 28.—At my Commentary; finished notes on Romans.

July 18.—Went to the Baptist Union (Welsh) at Ffestiniog; this year I gave the address from the chair.

July 22.—Returning on the Friday, I attended the funeral of Dr. Edwards, at Bala. A large number of ministers present.

Aug. 8.—Read the first proof of my Commentary on *Acts* xix., after a rest of ten years !

Oct. 29.—Wrote the history of Old Trosnant for January *Seren Gomer*.

Nov. 2.—Fearful reports of shipwrecks after the storms.

Dec. 31.—At my Commentary. Here ends 1887. " I praise Thee, O God." I preached on 28 Sundays this year.

**1888.** Jan. 1.—This year dawns badly for me—was very unwell all this month; suffered much from cold and hoarseness.

April 10. — Finished the Epistle of *Jude*; Rev. William Jones, of Nebo, Ebbw Vale, wrote most of the notes on *Revelation*. The last part came out on November 6th. I bless the Lord for help, and that I was permitted to see the end of my great work. Both Testaments are now complete.

April 18.—We removed to Riverston House, Caerleon Road.

May 7.—Wrote about "Cosmos" (in *South Wales Daily News*) to *Seren Cymru*.

June 5.—Wrote a paper to *Seren Cymru*.

June 27.—At Cwmdwr Association—my old home. I preached with much freedom.

July 10.—Preparing an article for the *Greal* on "The Present Time."

Dec. 5.—At the funeral of Rev. Nathaniel Thomas, of Cardiff; were together in college. He was a good minister of Christ.

During this year I visited many churches, far and near, to distribute my Commentary. I preached on 27 Sundays, and many times during the intervening weeks.

**1889.** Jan. 1.—"May the Lord be merciful to us this year."

April 2.—Began my journey to Carmarthen and Pembrokeshire to sell my Commentary; was from home nearly five weeks; preached nearly every night, and took a large number of orders for my work. During July, August, and September, I wrote largely for the *Seren Cymru* and the *Seren Gomer*.

Aug. 9.—At the annual meeting of the Bristol Baptist College.

Aug. 18.—Busy packing boxes for my daughter, Margaret Anne, who is going to India. She marries an American Baptist Missionary, named William Powell (a native of Abercarn), who is stationed at Nursaravapetta, in the Madras Presidency. May God bless them in their work!

Sept. 28 to Oct. 24.—This interval was occupied in a tour in North Wales, principally in Anglesea, selling my Commentary. I did fairly well.

My dear wife was very ill both during the rise and fall of this year; doubtless the parting with our youngest girl had much to do with it. I preached this year on 39 Sundays. Most of my time was occupied with the Commentary.

**1890.** Jan. 17.—Wrote a page to Cernyw for *Seren Gomer.*

Feb. 6.—A terrible explosion occurred at Llanerch Colliery, near Abersychan—180 lost their lives. There were some good men, and members of churches, among that number.

During March, wife and myself were poorly for some weeks, but the skilful treatment of Dr. Garrod Thomas brought us round.

March 18.—Wrote an article to the *Seren Cymru.*

April 16.—Sent a translation of Rev. W. Powell's letter (my son-in-law in India) to the *Seren Cymru.*

May 9.—Preparing for the Hebrew examination at Pontypool College.

May 23.—On examination papers for Haverfordwest College.

May 28. — At Blaenau Association; Rev. Evan Thomas and myself preached in Welsh.

June 12.—Wrote a short memoir of Rev. Daniel Jones, of Tongwynlais, to the *Seren Gomer.*

June 23.—Wrote a short paper to *Seren Cymru* on Rev. Robert Jones' book (of Llanllyfni) on Popery.

July 2.—Went on a fortnight's tour with my Commentary; visited several churches in Carmarthenshire, and did very well.

L

Aug. 9.—This year, again, I am sending to Dr. Booth, for the *Baptist Handbook*, memoirs of Welsh ministers.

Sept. 2.—Went to the Welsh Baptist Union at Swansea; from there to Aberystwyth and North Wales with my Commentary. Returned at end of the month much improved in health.

Oct. 7.—At the Baptist Union at Cardiff.

Oct. 8.—At the funeral of Mrs. Martha Williams, of Ebbw Vale, aged 59. She was buried at Bethlehem, Llanelly, where she was a member during my pastorate from 1856 to 1860. She was a genuine Christian. I buried her at her request.

Oct. 9.—My dear wife was again taken ill, and Dr. Garrod Thomas was again consulted. She got a little better, and on October 27th was able to go out shopping with our daughter Kate for a few hours. Alas! she never went out again until she was borne to her grave. On November 7th she had a kind of fit. When she came to herself, about 10 o'clock at night, I discovered that her mind was affected. On Sunday, the 9th, she had great head pain. On Tuesday night, the 11th, she finally took to her bed. Her pain ceased, but her left side was paralysed! She complained of weakness in that side; her eyes were dim, and she could not read. Though very quiet both day and night, and apparently free from pain, her mind was unhinged, and her speech had failed. She would alternately smile and weep. From Sunday, 23rd November, she sank rapidly; at midnight she was convulsed for a few seconds; from then to the end she was in a kind of sleep. Tuesday, 25th, our son Tom came from London. His dying mother opened her eyes and recognised him, and he was the last one she ever noticed. She died on the Thursday morning at 1.45. All through her illness she was calm and patient. We buried her at Newport Cemetery on December 1st, the chief mourners being my two eldest sons. Oh! what a trial this to me. Her age at death was 67. She had been a member 47 years, and we had walked together, step by step, nearly 39 years. "A loving wife, a tender mother, a sincere Christian." I must bow, and believe that all things work together for good to those who love Christ.

November.—I wrote a few letters to the *South Wales Daily News* anent Dr. Williams, a Romish priest at Cardiff.

December.—I had a severe attack of bronchitis, owing to exposure during my wife's illness, and was laid up six weeks.

During this year I preached on 34 Sabbaths, and many times during the weeks.

1891.—I feel quite unnerved; but I ventured to keep my engagement, and (Jan. 4th) preached twice at Ynyshir (Ferndale).

Jan. 11.—Preached twice for Rev. G. H. Cook at Summer Hill.

Jan. 14.—Sent a sermon of Mr. Richards' to the *Greal*.

Jan. 19.—Wrote a paper on Morgan Lloyd for the *Hauwr*.

Jan. 25.—My daughter Kate was baptized by Mr. Davies at Charles Street.

Jan. 31.—Wrote a letter to the *South Wales Daily News.*

Feb. 6 and 9.—Wrote papers for the *Seren Gomer.*

Feb. 10.—At the funeral of Mr. William Conway, at Pontrhydyrun; he was a relative of my wife.

Feb. 22.—Preached twice at Nebo, Ebbw Vale.

Feb. 25.—At our quarterly meeting, Llanwenarth.

March 1.—Preached at Cwmafon twice. Commentary well favored.

March 8.—Preached twice at Cross Keys (22), and twice at Neath.

April 5.—Preached twice at Ebenezer, Blaenavon, and (12) twice at Abercanaid; thence to Pendarren, returning through Pontypridd and Caerphilly.

Aug. 19.—A Sunday for Mrs. Lewis, widow of brother Lewis, of Troedyrhiw. Passed several copies of the Commentary.

April 26.—Preached at Carmel, Sirhowy; baptized two in the new baptistery (now used for the first time).

April 29.—Wrote a long, helping letter to Rev. Johns, of Neyland, in connection with his work now in hand.

May 5.—Placed a granite tombstone on my wife's grave.

May 10.—Preached at Nebo, Ebbw Vale. My daughter Kate accompanied me there; she was the guest of Mrs. Wilputte.

May 12.—At Examination papers in Hebrew of Pontypool students.

May 13.—My daughter Kate and self visited Bath Flower Show.

May 15.—Death of old Mr. Williams, at the age of 80—a deacon at Charles Street; a true Christian.

May 19 and 20.—At the annual meetings of Pontypool College.

May 24.—Preached twice for Mr. Cocker, Pontnewydd.

May 27 and 28.—Our Association was held at Commercial Road Chapel, Newport. Personally, I enjoyed but little of the services, as I was suffering from severe cough.

June 7.—Preached twice at Cefn; communion.

June 11.—At the funeral of my old friend, Mr. Llew. Richards—a prominent member and deacon at the Temple.

June 14.—Preached twice at Tabor, Brynmawr; communion.

June 17.—My son Percy came home suddenly from Sydney. It was quite a surprise visit; we had not heard of his coming.

June 21.—Preached twice at Castleton.

June 25.—Removed to Morden Road; Percy greatly helped us.

June 27.—Preached twice at Llanthewy; glad to revisit my first church.

June 29.—Percy bade adieu to us, and left for London, *en route* to New South Wales. He feels the loss of his mother acutely.

July 5.—Preached twice at Frogmore Street, Abergavenny.

July 12.—Preached twice at Beulah. (19th) Twice at Salem, Cardiff; communion. (26th) Twice at Salem, Blaenau.

Aug. 2.—Preached twice at Llanwenarth; communion.

Aug. 9.—At Nebo, Ebbw Vale, twice; was entertained by Mr. Wilputte.

Aug. 13.—At Pontypool House and Central Committee.

Aug. 16.—Preached twice at Charles Street Chapel, Newport.

Aug. 21.—At the funeral of Rev. D. Edwards, 76, Calvinist Methodist minister.

Aug. 23.—Preached at Llysfaen. 24th, At Ordination of Mr. Edwards, at Beulah. 26th, At quarterly meeting, Tabernacle, Pontypool.

Aug. 30.—Preached twice at Llantarnam; communion.

Sept. 1-3.—At Baptist Union, Carmarthen; thence I went to Llanwrtyd Wells, where I preached twice. Visited Talgarth; preached at Maesyberllan; walked over to Tredustan, the scene of my school-days in 1843.

Sept. 14.—At home preparing the memoir of Rev. James Michael Ponthir for the *Seren Gomer*. 27th, Preached at Maesteg.

October.—During this month I preached at Llanelly (Brec.), my second church; heard Dr. Culross at Stow Hill, Newport; was much hindered at work through being very poorly during greater part of this month and November, which is answerable for a large number of deaths. Not much fine weather all through harvest-time—crops failing generally. Prepared a paper on Rev. D. Richards, Caerphilly, for the *Greal*.

**1892.** January.—During this month I preached but twice. I was in indifferent health, and the weather was bad. I spent much of my time in reading the history of the early Baptists, and their sufferings in time of persecution.

Feb. 1.—The great C. H. Spurgeon died last night at Mentone; he was God's gift to His Church for a long time. Wrote a continuation of Spurgeon's life for the second edition of his sermons. Read much of old Baptist history; preached five times, and attended several committees—Pontypool, Cefn, &c.

March.—Wrote a paper on "Welsh Old Baptists" for *Seren Cymru*. Preached only thrice during this month. I feel weak and poorly, and am often with Dr. Thomas. Weather very unfavourable for me. On 31st I went to Cefn, to the recognition services of Rev. T. G. James.

April.—I preached seven times during this month. Visited Cilfynydd, Gelli, Penuel, Rhymney, Tirzah, and other places, selling my Commentary. I found a little gardening healthful.

May.—Preached six times during this month. Visited Pontypool, Newbridge—where our Association meetings were held—Goytre. Wrote papers on Miles Edwards for the *Hauwr*, and on Llanwenarth for the *Baptist*.

June.—Preached at Ebenezer and Horeb, Blaen-avon; also at Croesyparc. The first sermon I preached in old Horeb was in 1884. Wrote some matter to Rev. D. Powell, Liverpool, furnishing him with some data for his history of "Cymro Bach."

July.—I have reason to bless the Lord for much help in weakness—that through all I have been enabled to keep up to my work. Preached, and held two communion services at Frogmore Street, Abergavenny. Preached at Cross Keys; at Carmel, Sirhowy; visited Lancaster (the home of my son Neander), and preached twice at Salem, Cardiff, on my way home.

August.—Preached sermons at Castleton, the Tabernacle, Cardiff, Llanwenarth. Visited Pontypool College (Committees) during this month.

September.—Preached at Ynysybwl, Carmel, Sirhowy, Tylorstown, and Maerdy, where I disposed, in each case, of a number of copies of my Commentary. An extraordinary meeting of Pontypool College was held to consider the removal of the institution to Cardiff. Fifty-three voted for the transmigration, and 43 were against such change. Alas! for the old establishment. At the time I thought it was a great blunder, but I have somewhat modified my opinion since.

October.—Was largely occupied in itinerating with my Commentary. (I should like to finish at it, as I feel my health failing.) I preached at Hollybush (with Brother Edwards, of Beulah), at Glanaman, Llansamlet, and Swansea.

November.—Preached at Cowbridge twice; also twice at Magor. The Lord gave me much help. Wrote to *Seren Cymru* a ventilation of my opinion *re* our college.

December.—Preached at Salem (an offshoot of Cardiff), Llanelly, my old church, and Bethesda,

Swansea. This has been to me a merciful year—free from heavy sickness, and I have not wanted "any good thing." I praise the Lord, and pray for pardon for all faults.

1893.—"O Lord, be very gracious to me this year again." Very cold weather and hard frost usher in this New Year. Preached only three times during January.

February.—Heard Dr. Lees at the Temperance Hall. Preached at Nebo, Ebbw Vale, and Charles Street, Newport. Wrote the history of our College for the *Seren Gomer.*

March.—My son-in-law (Rev. William Powell), with his wife and two boys, arrived from their station on the Indian Mission Field. They stayed nearly two years. Preached at Salem, Blaenau, and at Bethel, Llanelly (Carmarthen).

April.—Preached at Brynaman, Moriah, Risca (my last pastorate), Blaenau Gwent. Here a tablet to the memory of the old minister, Rev. John Lewis, was unveiled. He had ministered to this church 44 years; he was a good old brother who preached with "hwyl."

May.—On the 2nd inst. my daughter and her husband sailed to America to visit the head-quarters of the American Baptist Missionary Society, returning after an absence of ten weeks. I preached at Cardiff, Tynewydd, and at our Association at Sirhowy. The annual meeting of our College was held for the last time at Pontypool. Large crowds were there.

June.—Dr. Culross, of Bristol, preached an excellent sermon at Summer Hill (Newport) Association. I

wrote a letter on the Telugu Mission to *Seren Cymru.*
Mr. Richard Jones, of Govilon, was buried at Llan-
wenarth. He was a son of my dear old friend,
William Jones, of Cwmmera.

July.—I visited, on the 5th inst., our dear old
brother, Rev. Evan Thomas, at the Newport In-
firmary. He had met with an accident, and I fear
his end is near. I have been unable to preach much ;
am still under doctor's care.

August.—I went to Llanwrtyd Wells for a change—
am 70 on the 4th inst.—returned a little improved.
Preached twice at Bethlehem, Llanelly, and thrice at
Tongwynlais, though still very weak. Preached twice
at Llanwenarth ; communion. Translated a letter of
Rev. W. Powell's for *Seren Cymru.*

September.—Rev. Evan Thomas, of Newport, died
on the 5th, and was buried in the presence of a large
congregation on the 8th, at Newport Cemetery.

October.—I preached on all Sundays this month—
at Pisgah, and at the Temple, Newport.

November.—Wrote a short history of Rev. D. D.
Evans, of Pontrhydyrun, for the *Greal ;* examined the
MSS. of *Nefydd.* On the 22nd, a dear old friend—Mr.
Jenkins, of Argoed—was laid to rest. He was one of
our old standards.

December.—Preached at Goytre and at Bethel,
Bassalleg. Heard (5th) Professor Barbier (French
tutor at Cardiff University) *trying* to lecture on Wales ;
his English was awfully bad !

I praise the Lord for His help this year. This has
been very bad for trade ; very many have suffered

want owing to the conflict between capital and labour; much remains still to be settled.

During this year I preached on 31 Sundays.

**1894.**—The bad weather of January prevented my leaving home often, and consequently I did little preaching; Newport and Treherbert were the only places visited. I did much reading, which compensated in a measure.

February.—Among other items this month, I wrote a long letter *re* Christmas Evans to Dr. Owen Davies, Carnarvon.

March.—Preached at Cross Keys. Translated a paper on the Telugu Mission, on behalf of Rev. W. Powell, for *Seren Cymru.*

April.—Preached at the English Baptist Church, Treherbert, Llanwenarth, and at Lion Street, Abergavenny.

May.—Preached at Cwmbwrla, near Swansea; at Dinas, and at Clydach. At our Association meetings at Cross Keys, where some good sermons in English and Welsh were preached.

June.—Preached for the English Baptists at Treherbert, at Bethel, Bassalleg, and at Pontrhydyrun. At Cardiff (late Pontypool) College meetings (13th).

July.—Conducted two communion services at Ponthir. Preached at Cefn, Cross Keys, and at Glascoed during the month.

August.—On the 5th I preached twice at the Tabernacle, Cardiff, these being special memorial services. I preached there 50 years before with the Blind Preacher of Swansea. I preached from the same text as the blind man and I had at that time. 29th, I preached on a special subject selected for me at Calvary, Brynmawr.

September.—I wrote a paper for the *Seren Cymru* on old Jenkin Harris, an itinerant preacher 50 years ago. Visited Pontycymmer, near Bridgend, and Bargoed.

October.—Preached during this month at Dinas, Merthyr, also at Bethel, Briton Ferry, and Tongwynlais. Heard the Rev. Newman Hall at the Tabernacle, Newport; excellent sermon and sound doctrine. Though 80 years of age, the doctor looked strong and well.

November.—My son-in-law and daughter returned to their Mission work at Nursaravapetta. This month was much occupied with writing papers.

I praise the Lord for all His kindness to me and mine through the year. May those who have just returned to India have a safe voyage; may blessing rest upon them and their Mission work.

1895.—January opened cold and with very hard frost, which continued into February, on 18th of which month Rev. Wyndham Lewis, Calvinist Methodist minister, of Carmarthen, and his wife died within a few hours of each other. Dr. Briscoe, of Holyhead, a clergyman and very learned man, died at a very old age. I had had some acquaintance with him; he once gave me some of his printed Hebrew translations of Scripture. 26th, Lord Aberdare died, aged 82.

April 4.—Rev. William Jones and myself attended the funeral of Dr. Edward Roberts, Pontypridd; there was a very large assembly. 14th, I preached twice at Libanus, Treherbert. 17th, Wrote on Popery in Wales to the *Seren Cymru.*

June.—On the 2nd preached at Raglan and Kincoed. Mr. Johnson, the old minister, is dead. 12th, Went to Carmarthen to the funeral of Rev. Mr. Roberts, my successor at Peniel. I and another minister preached in the chapel the same evening. Mr. Roberts was a good brother.

July.—On the 22nd attended Sir William Harcourt's great meeting at Abertillery; thousands were there, and the enthusiasm was great.

Sept. 7.—Accompanied by my daughter, I made my last visit to London. I did not preach on this occasion; but I heard Rev. H. E. Stone at St. John's Wood, and Rev. C. W. Vick at Brondesbury Chapel. Went to see Spurgeon's Monument at Norwood Cemetery; very solemn to me. Visited Earl's Court, and the " Big Wheel."

Sept. 26.—Heard Dean Farrar at the Temperance Hall, Newport, where there was a full audience. The Dean is a superior man in every way; he spoke well and pathetic. No striving for oratory; most interesting and instructive.

Oct. 3.—Visited the new Electric Lighting Station on the occasion of the starting of the plant—grand and intricate !

Nov. 6.—Heard the Jesuit Gerard, at Tredegar Hall —subject, " The Gunpowder Plot." I made a few remarks on his lecture in the *South Wales Argus.* Catholics will deny anything if it is against them.

Nov. 14.—Heard the venerable Mr. Müller, of Bristol (91 years of age), at Cardiff. For an hour-and-a-half he gave a wonderful discourse, which was full of rare faith.

December.—Much of this month was occupied in writing. I preached on one Sunday at my old church, Moriah.

**1896.** Jan. 8.—Rev. James Johns, of Horeb, Blaenavon—a good young man, and a hard worker—was buried at his old home at Pembroke. 10th, Benjamin Williams, an important officer in Cefn Church, was found drowned in the feeder near his house. It was feared that difficulty in business had led to suicide. 16th, At the Welsh National Liberal Association at the Temperance Hall. *Parturient Montes, &c.* 26th, Heard Dr. A. T. Pierson at Stow Hill Chapel—a very able preacher.

March 2.—Prepared a paper for *Seren Gomer* on William Hopkin, the helper of "Mathetes" in his dictionary. 19th, Heard a thrilling lecture on Armenian Atrocities at the Temperance Hall—truly awful. 31st, Mr. T. H. Thomas (son of the late Dr. Thomas, Pontypool) lectured in the Town Hall on "Early Italian Art," illustrated with colored slides.

April.—Reading Jones' History of the Baptists in Radnorshire. Wrote a paper to *Seren Cvmru* on Samuel Jones, a Jamaica Missionary. Preached at Horeb, Blaenavon, Libanus, Treherbert, and on a week night for Mr. Cook, Summer Hill.

May.—At our Association at Blaenavon ; best of all was Mathias of Sirhowy, who died soon after.

May 31.—Rev. J. G. Greenhough preached at Stow Hill—good, as he usually is.

June.—Visited Brecon; preached at Kensington and Watergate; on to Senny Bridge and Devynock—familiar places—and at Maesyberllan Association. Thence to Llandovery, Llanwrtyd, and Llangammarch (where I preached), returning *via* Hereford to Newport.

July.—Preached for the new cause at Senghenydd, near Caerphilly, at Ebbw Vale, and Castleton. At our Baptist Union meetings at Pontypridd.

August.—Copied Christmas Evans' letters for Dr. O. Davies. Preached at Treherbert, Cefn, and at Crane Street, Pontypool.

September.—Dr. Owen Davies and I preached at my old church at Carmarthen. Preached at Horeb, Cwmdwr (my old home), at Raglan, Kincoed, and Llanwenarth.

November.—On the 1st, preached at my old church at Carmarthen; communion. I caught severe cold on this trip, and suffered for going so far in such weather as then prevailed. Sent my paper on Rev. J. P. Davies to the *Greal*. Wrote to the *Seren Cymru re* Rev. Fletcher, of Madeley. 19th, At the re-opening of Old Frogmore Street Chapel, Abergavenny. Wrote on the Papacy for the *Star of Gwent*; I gave the substance of Gavazzi's orations. 17th, A sharp shock of earthquake took place; it was felt by a great many. 31st, Good Dr. Herber Evans died—a great preacher and speaker.

Here I close another year's work. I preached only on 19 Sundays; I have had fairly good health, though

I feel my sun going down. I have written much—several letters on Popery to the *Seren Cymru.*

**1897.**—Rheumatism troubles me much—weather being cold and damp. Was at the funeral of Mr. Bevan, an old friend.

February to April.—I was out but very little ; laid by much with rheumatism, but God has been my Helper.

May.—On 18th my dear old brother, W. Davies (formerly of Tredegar), died, and was buried at Tredegar.

June 16-17.—At our Annual College Meetings at Cardiff. The Queen's Jubilee is now the uppermost thing all over the world. How soon even this will pass away !

June.—While at Llanwrtyd Wells I read the memoir of Rev. David Williams, former Independent Minister at Gelynos—the plain old sanctuary just over the Wells. I knew him well, and heard him several times ; he was a popular preacher, and nearly 100 years old when he passed away.

August.—On Sunday, 1st, heard " Eifionydd " preach at Mount Zion, Newport ; good matter, but not much energy. The speaker appeared weak and worn. The great event of this week was the National Eisteddfod. Although thousands of pounds were received from all sources, and the weather was all that could be desired, there was yet a great deficit. On Sunday, 8th, I heard the venerable Bard and Druid (now Archdruid), Hwfa Mon, preach at Mount Zion Chapel. He was very good and Puritanical ; his theme was prayer.

September.—In company with my daughter Kate, I made a farewell visit to Abergavenny, Llanelly (Brec.), and Brynmawr.

October.—Was much occupied in writing and translations for *Seren Cymru*. I also prepared a paper on Rev. Thomas Jenkins, of Bristol, for same journal. At the re-opening of Charles Street Chapel, Newport, on 31st.

November.—A Sabbath morning at Summer Hill Chapel; a week evening with Dr. Edwards, at Cardiff; at Dr. Dallinger's illustrated lecture on " Beauty considered in Minute Nature." These were some of the ways I spent this month.

December.—Some of the doings of this month were :—A visit to the College, Cardiff; sent an old funeral sermon, *re* Rev. Francis Hiley, to the *Greal*; preached twice at Cefn; twice at my old church at Risca; heard a good lecture on Müller by Rev. C. Davies, of Cardiff, at the Temple, Newport, &c. Here ends another year. I bless the Lord for His lovingkindness and continued help. This year has tried me much. Since 1840, when I began to speak for the Master, I have not had a year like this. Have preached fewest times ! May the Lord in His love grant me strength and moderate health till He sees it time to call me away to Himself.

1898.—I have little to record this year.

April 14.—Heard Dr. Nansen at the Drill Hall on his voyage to the North Pole. 18th, At the re-opening of Rev. Pardoe Thomas's Chapel, with new organ. He had ministered for many years; now his health has entirely failed.

M

May.—At an anti-gambling meeting (4th) at Tredegar Hall—a very large attendance. My son-in-law and my daughter (who was in very poor health) arrived from India; she will have a long furlough. 19th, Heard with dismay this morning of the death of the Right Hon. William Ewart Gladstone.

June.—Preached at the Tabernacle, Merthyr. At the meetings of the general assembly of Welsh Calvinistic Methodists; excellent throughout.

September.—On the 1st the colliers' strike ended; it has lasted five months, and was a terrible loss to South Wales in particular. 5th, At the funeral of Rev. Mr. Ayliffe, of St. Mary Street; thousands of people lined the streets to pay their last respects to one who was truly a disciple of the Good Shepherd. Wrote a letter to the *Baptist* re Bishop Hedley's " Pastoral." May Heaven defend us from these Papists and Ritualists! At the Convention at the Temperance Hall; preached twice at Cefn.

November.—Sent memoirs of Rev. John Williams. Llandovery, to *Seren Cymru*; also that of Rev. D. Jones, Cwmsarnddu, and Rev. J. Morgan, Talrhyn. to same paper. Memoir of Rev. T. Gabriel Jones to the *Seren Gomer*.

December.—On 8th, visited Mrs. Timothy Thomas : she died on 10th, and was buried on 13th in her husband's grave. Her age was 88. On the 14th, I gave a short address at Cefn monthly meeting on " The Holy Spirit in the Church." I was unable to leave home much this year. I preached about four times, but wrote largely for the Press. May the Lord help me a little longer!

**1899.**—During the early part of the year I assisted Mr. Rees, of Granant, on his " History of Blaenywaun and its Branches." (It was published end of this year in a neat vol., cloth, 1s. 6d.)

June 5.—At the Centenary of Siloh, Tredegar. 21st, At our College annual meetings at Cardiff.

August. — Visited Llanwrtyd Wells, to which I said—" Farewell."

December.—I did not preach but four times during this year, being too unwell to go from home. I did little work of any kind, and feel all my toil and labour is now over. The Lord has been merciful to me and mine. Praise to His great Name. Amen.

The great curse at the end of this year was the terrible war in South Africa. Lord, let it end! This will be no glory to England; it ought never to have been begun. For a while the battles went against us, and there was terrible slaughter.

*Appendix.*

(By C. E. L.)

DURING the year 1900 my dear father's health decidedly declined. He preached but little, wrote occasionally for the *Seren Cymru*, and attended with regularity the committees and annual meetings of his Alma Mater at Cardiff. He also took a deep interest in all meetings held in and around Newport in connection with the Free Churches, and all matters relating to Temperance. Throughout his life he was a total abstainer, and in the early years of his ministry was a staunch advocate of Juvenile and Adult Temperance Societies—at a period when to be a teetotaler was not so popular as to-day.

At home he was a disciplinarian—and withal the kindest of fathers. Both father and mother were strict observers of the Day of Rest: we were trained early to attend the House of God, and to love the Sunday School. My brother Tom began teaching before he was 14, and (among other " veteran " teachers in Wales) was awarded a diploma of honour by the Sunday School Union in October, 1901, on the completion of 25 years' service.

Since dear mother's death—which took place just ten years, almost to the day, before that of my father —I had been his almost constant companion. His activity and patience were marvellous ; he was systematic almost to a fault; he did everything day by day; his diary in the *Welsh Baptist Handbook* had been religiously kept for a large number of years—even down to the day before his death my father had entered his "log." Within the pages of these *Hand-books* (which are now in the library of the Baptist College at Cardiff) are recorded many events which will doubtless be invaluable for reference to generations of students yet to come.

In the foregoing pages of the autobiography it will be observed that the reader is referred to cuttings from magazines, periodicals, and the daily and weekly press. My father was much interested in the preservation of reports of important events bearing on Baptist and Nonconformist propaganda, and matters of even a wider interest. He invariably cut out and filed these reports, and they are also in the College Library, under the vigilant eye of Dr. Edwards.

It was a source of great joy to my father that his health was spared in such complete measure until the consummation of his life-work—the "Commentary on the Bible." Not only was the work completed and printed, but nearly every copy had been sold before the author's death. I join with him in the hope that God will bless the "Esboniad," and that it will be a source of help to many a Bible student.

Father had one or two serious attacks of illness during the last years, and the year 1900 showed a decided decay of the house of clay. The dreadful South African War weighed heavily on his heart, for he was a man of peace, and when reading the daily

reports he would groan and sigh over " deeds that will
bring us no honor, and which ought never to have
been begun."

He always took deep interest in, and was ever ready
to help country churches. I have many a time known
him start off, in bad weather, on a Saturday night, or
early on Sunday morning, on foot, to Blackwood,
or elsewhere, to fill the pulpit of a brother minister
who, through illness, or some other cause, was unable
to preach. With the men who earn their bread in
the bowels of the earth he was in deep sympathy. I
well recollect father returning home from a long
journey on the day after the terrible colliery explosion
at Abercarn; without a moment's delay he posted off
to see what help he could render.

While we were at Carmarthen he was truly a friend
of the fishermen, and more than one petition did he
get up, and lay before the Home Office, on behalf of
those who " go down to the sea in ships."

It was on November 11th, 1900, while on a visit to
Cefn Chapel, Tydu (and where he was a member), that
father caught the last cold which ended in his death
three weeks later. He had a long-cherished desire
that God would not allow him to linger, and be a
burden to anyone. That prayer was granted. For
many months before his death his well-known figure
was regularly seen at Summer Hill Chapel, where he
much enjoyed the preaching of Rev. G. H. Cook, for
whom he sometimes deputised. He was present at
Summer Hill on the morning of his last Sabbath but
one on earth (Nov. 25th); he was even out of doors

three days later, but the cardiac asthma from which he was suffering got the better of him; he took to his bed on Saturday, December 1st, and passed away peacefully on the Sunday night. Thus he was born on a Sunday, the 3rd of the month; expired on Sunday, the 2nd.

## THE FUNERAL.

In the Newport Cemetery—beautiful for situation— we laid him to rest on Wednesday afternoon, December 5th, in the grave made for our mother, and where she sleeps.

It was a wretchedly cold and wet day, but a large number of ministers, deacons, and church members came to pay their last tribute. Addresses were delivered in the Cemetery Chapel by Rev. T. Thomas, Risca; Rev. D. Bevan Jones, Caerleon; Rev. C. Davies, of Cardiff; and (at the graveside) by Rev. T. G. James, Tydu; and Rev. D. Davies, Charles Street Church, Newport. Prayer was offered by Rev. Professor Davies, M.A., of Cardiff, and Rev. J. George, of Magor.

Principal Edwards, D.D., of Cardiff, delivered an address full of eulogy, in which he said that the deceased possessed some of the noblest traits that could be discerned in any man, and that he had a rare combination of excellencies which produced an all-roundness and perfection of character. Mr. Patagonia Lewis attended as a special representative of Penuel, Carmarthen; and others who were present included Mr. W. Edwards, J.P., Maindee; Mr. T.

Phillips, J.P., Rev. J. P. Davies, Caerphilly; Revs. William Jones, J. M. Jones, D. Evans, G. Evans, T. Williams, A. T. Jones, H. Abraham, all of Newport; Rev. J. Williams, of Brynmawr, and Rev. T. Williams, Nantyglo.

The *South Wales Daily News, South Wales Argus, Seren Cymru, Christian World, Baptist Times* (in which was a portrait), and the *Baptist* current numbers contain full accounts of father's life, and which doubtless have been seen and read.

The coffin was carried by members of Tydu Church, and bore the following inscription :—

In loving memory of

Rev. THOMAS LEWIS, Newport (Mon.),

Who died Dec. 2nd, 1900,

Aged 77 years.

Laid to rest in Newport Cemetery, Dec. 5th,

"Till the Trumpet shall sound."

"I have fought a good fight; I have finished my course
I have kept the faith."

Thus ended the life begun on August 3rd, 1823. His children "rise up and call him blessed." His was a praiseful life from the beginning to the end; praise is the keynote and the finale of "My Life's History."

I think it was the late C. H. Spurgeon who, in one of his very last addresses, said, "The vista of a praiseful life will never cease, but will continue throughout eternity; from psalm to psalm, from hallelujah to hallelujah, we will climb the hill of the Lord till we reach the Holiest of All, where with veiled faces we will bow before the Divine Majesty in the bliss of endless adoration ! "

I trust that the foregoing autobiography, in diary form, will be found both pleasant and profitable reading. I have omitted nothing from the original MS. which could possibly be of public interest and service, and, at the same time, render the reading as pithy as might be.

My most grateful thanks are due to Principal Edwards, D.D., of Cardiff Baptist College, for his kindness in the revision of the work; to Rev. William Jones, and other reverend gentlemen, who have collaborated in the production of the work, without whose help it would have been impossible to produce the autobiography which I hope will meet with the approval of subscribers and friends who have thus also, in a marked manner, assisted me in this labour of love.

CATHERINE E. LEWIS.

220, CHEPSTOW ROAD,
     NEWPORT, MON.

---

N.B.—As only one edition is printed, and the number of copies limited, early application is advised —to above address.

www.ingramcontent.com/pod-product-compliance
Ingram Content Group UK Ltd.
Pitfield, Milton Keynes, MK11 3LW, UK
UKHW052136151224
452458UK00010B/108